THE HEART OF VIRTUE

DONALD DE MARCO

THE HEART OF VIRTUE

Lessons
from
Life and Literature
Illustrating
the
Beauty and Value of
Moral Character

IGNATIUS PRESS   SAN FRANCISCO

Cover by Riz Boncan Marsella

© 1996 Ignatius Press, San Francisco
ISBN 0–89870–568–1
Library of Congress catalogue number 95–79949
Printed in the United States of America ⊗

When wealth is lost,
   nothing is lost;
When health is lost,
   something is lost;
When character is lost,
   all is lost.

          — Anonymous

Talent is nurtured in
solitude; character is
formed in the stormy
billows of the world.

          — Goethe

The virtues of great
men served me as a modern
mirror in which I might
adorn my own life.

          — Plutarch

Finally, brethren, whatever
is true, whatever is
honorable, whatever is just,
whatever is pure, whatever
is lovely, whatever is gracious,
if there is any excellence,
if there is anything
worthy of praise, think about
these things.

          — Saint Paul

To Peggy Markell
and
Tadeusz van Wollen
for their
clear insight,
kind inspiration,
and
gentle insistence

Contents

Acknowledgment (11)
Prologue (13)
Care (19)
Chastity (26)
Compassion (34)
Courage (42)
Courtesy (49)
Determination (56)
Faith (62)
Fidelity (69)
Generosity (77)
Graciousness (83)
Gratitude (91)
Holiness (99)
Hope (105)
Humility (113)
Integrity (122)
Justice (130)
Loyalty (137)
Meekness (144)
Mercy (151)
Mirthfulness (158)
Modesty (165)
Patience (172)
Piety (181)

Prudence (189)
Reverence (196)
Sincerity (204)
Temperance (212)
Wisdom (220)
Epilogue (229)

Acknowledgment

IT WAS STORMY. That and my flight schedule (Hartford-Springfield to Toronto to Calgary, Alberta, to Kamloops, British Columbia), with its minimal intervals between flights, seemed a most fitting way to celebrate the spirit of National Stress Awareness Day, April 16, 1994.

Almost predictably, "inclement enroute weather" delayed the arrival of Flight #1473 into Toronto. As a result, I was unable to make my connecting flight to Calgary. The best the airline could do for me was to send me to Vancouver, put me up in a hotel, and fly me to Kamloops the next day.

While waiting for the plane that would take me to Vancouver (which was two hours late from Paris), I was wondering what better plans the Great Scheduler in the Sky might have for me. Faith can be a wonderful aid in the management of stress.

I was seated in the departure lounge when I recognized a friend who lives in Vancouver. He also recognized me. We had spoken to each other two or three times after talks I had given in that city, and, although we had shared a number of common enthusiasms on those occasions, we could not consider ourselves to be close friends. So I was not offended when he said to me: "You know, I don't think of you often." I was, however, surprised to hear what followed: "But I did think of you just yesterday while in Miami. I had an inspiration that you should write a book about moral virtues, and that you should illustrate it with memorable stories from life and from literature." This revelation was all the more extraordinary because on that same day I had received a letter from a woman in up-state New York who also urged me to write the very same book. In fact, I had brought her letter with me for good luck.

There were other coincidences of a similarly startling nature. I asked my friend to tell me his seat assignment. As it turned out, we had been assigned adjacent seats! During the five-hour flight we talked about what virtues should go into the book, how they should be exemplified, and about divine synchronicity.

"Synchronicity is God's way of remaining anonymous", someone once said. That may be the case in more instances than we realize. One must be evergrateful for God's Providence. But concerning this specific instance, I want to take the opportunity now provided me to express my gratitude to my two friends, for, without their gentle insistence, *The Heart of Virtue* would not exist.

September 28, 1995
Kitchener, Ontario

Prologue

I T IS NOT POSSIBLE to improve either our personal lives or our society apart from acquiring virtue. We are reluctant to do this, however, because we believe that our sole moral responsibility is to eliminate vice, which we think we can accomplish with a minimum of effort. Yet we lull ourselves into a dangerous moral complacency when we assume that vice is no more formidable a foe than a draft of cold air that we can keep out by slamming the door in its face. It is equally perilous to maintain that slogans are sufficiently powerful to keep the devil at bay. Just saying "no" to drugs, racism, prejudice, and all forms of sexual aggression does not transform them into gentle lambs that will obediently go away even if our "no" does mean "no". Vices therefore invade and inhabit our lives. And while we fail to discern their lingering presence, we do remain outraged by crime. Yet crime is nothing less than the unseemly dividend that vice had always promised.

Saying "no" to vice and voicing indignation at crime logically presupposes the presence in us of positive and protecting virtues. But we often take these virtues for granted even when we have done nothing to understand, acquire, or develop them. Trying to become virtuous merely by excluding vice, however, is as unrealistic as trying to cultivate roses solely by eliminating weeds. After clearing the garden of weeds, one must still plant seeds or cuttings and nurture their growth; otherwise, the weeds simply return. The best way to exclude vices is to crowd them out with the presence of strong virtues. If we oppose crime, we must oppose vice, and if we oppose vice, we must promote virtue. Clifton Fadiman's maxim is worth repeating: "The formula for Utopia on earth remains always the same: to make a necessity of virtue."

Where strong virtues are lacking, the vices that rush in to fill the void often assume the mask of virtue. Dorothy Sayers has her own list of such counterfeit virtues, which she calls the "Seven Deadly Virtues". They are: Respectability, Childishness, Mental Timidity, Dullness, Sentimentality, Censoriousness, and Depression of Spirits.[1] Sayers is mindful of how easy it has been for human beings throughout the ages to pervert the seven foundational virtues into seven hapless imitations. The seven virtues that are the cornerstone of the moral life consist of three theological virtues—Faith, Hope, and Love—along with the four cardinal virtues of Prudence, Justice, Fortitude, and Temperance. The first three, sometimes called "supernatural virtues", are infused at baptism and correspond to the life of grace; while the cardinal virtues, although not entirely removed from sources of grace, are their more naturalistic counterparts. The theological virtues give us a focus that transcends us without excluding us. In this way they are the perfect antidotes to self-centeredness and its consequent vice, pride. The cardinal virtues, sometimes called "the Human Virtues", give us a focus within ourselves that does not exclude others—a self-mastery for the purpose of self-giving. The Seven Deadly Imitations that more closely parallel these seven virtues as

[1] Dorothy Sayers, *Creed or Chaos?* (London: Methuen, 1947), p. 23.

their sinister opposites are, respectively, Credulity, Expectation, Sentimentality, Cleverness, Legalism, Recklessness, and Tepidity. These mockeries of virtue more closely resemble the Seven Deadly Sins—Pride, Avarice, Envy, Wrath, Lust, Gluttony, and Sloth—which are wholly destructive of personality.

We are not born virtuous. Nature does not steep us in good habits. Nor does moral development take place by means of cultural osmosis. Virtues must be pursued.

> Ye were not formed to live the life of brutes,
> But virtue to pursue and knowledge high.[2]

It is precisely the vigorous pursuit, acquisition, and cultivation of virtues that enable us to conquer vice. Falling into vice is as easy as falling off a ladder. To acquire virtue, however, is more arduous. "The life of sin is a fall from coherence to chaos," according to Saint Thomas Aquinas, "the life of virtue a climb from the many to the One."[3]

The notion of virtue as a slow, methodical ascent also appears in the writings of Saint Augustine. In a celebrated passage, he says, "We make a ladder out of our vices if we trample the vices under foot."[4] Henry Wadsworth Longfellow wrote a poetic tribute to this Augustinian phrase that includes the following stanza:

> We have not wings, we cannot soar;
> But we have feet to scale and climb

[2] Dante Alighieri, "Inferno", *The Divine Comedy,* trans. by Henry F. Cary, canto 26, pp. 116–17.

[3] Thomas Aquinas, *Summa Theologiae,* I–II, 73, 1.

[4] Augustine, "Sermon no. 176, On the Ascension of the Lord", in J. P. Migne (ed.), *Patrologiae Latinae* (1845), vol. 38:949 "De vitiis nostris scalam nobis facimus, si vitia ipsa calcamus."

> By slow degrees, by more and more,
> The cloudy summits of our time.[5]

Virtue and vice are adversaries. Indeed, they are locked in mortal combat with each other. No virtue is complete that has not been victorious in its struggle with its corresponding vice. The virtuous person advances by crushing vices under his feet. It is in this context that we begin to appreciate the positive and even heroic quality that virtue possesses. Far from being merely good manners or social affectations, virtue is really the perfection of the human person on the highest level of his being—his moral worth, which is to say, his humanity.

Love is not simply one virtue among others, but the form of all virtues. Each virtue finds its essential humanity and its nobility in the love that animates it. Conversely, love would be impotent if it were not for the various virtues that withstand attendant difficulties and deliver their message of love where love is needed. Love is deed; virtue is the conduit that delivers love. Just as fire hoses are needed to convey and direct water from its source to where the fire rages, virtue is needed to establish a connective between the source of love and the place where love is needed. No person, no matter how loving he claims to be, can be of any help to himself or anyone else on a moral level if he does not possess virtue. A soldier without courage, a doctor without care, a teacher without patience, a parent without prudence, a spouse without fidelity, a priest without faith, a leader without determination, a magistrate without integrity, and a friend without

---

[5] Henry Wadsworth Longfellow, "The Ladder of Saint Augustine", in *Favorite Poems: Henry Wadsworth Longfellow* (Garden City, N.Y.: Doubleday, 1947), p. 304.

loyalty are all partners to futility, not because they lack love, but because they lack the virtue to express it.

Twenty-eight virtues have been selected to describe twenty-eight different ways love can be expressed. According to ancient mathematicians, twenty-eight is a perfect number because it is the sum of its divisors $(1 + 2 + 4 + 7 + 14)$. Among two-digit numbers, only twenty-eight is "perfect". Thus, it is an appropriate number to use in describing powers that are perfective of men.

Each virtue is presented in the context of stories taken from life or from literature. The purpose here is to allow the moral value of each virtue to have a more immediate appeal. Since virtues reside primarily in personal actions, rather than in the mind, these stories better represent the "heart of virtue". At the same time, it is important to understand the distinctive nature of each virtue and how the virtues relate to each other to form an organic or "symphonic" whole. Therefore, each chapter has a philosophical commentary that helps to sharpen and refine the identity and complementarity of the twenty-eight virtues presented. Thus, virtue is presented to the reader in an immediate and intuitive manner, as well as in one that is discursive and intellectual.

The virtuous person is a person of character, a whole person, a fully realized person. Virtue, as Plato has taught, is the health, strength, and excellence of a soul in communion with reality. It is virtue more than anything else that fills a person with a sense of himself, his vitality, his purpose, and his happiness.

CARE

THE FIRST MEETING between Karol Wojtyla and Padre Pio took place in 1947. The twenty-seven-year-old Pole, recently ordained, had journeyed to San Giovanni Rotondo, hoping that the world-famous Capuchin friar would hear his confession. What exactly the two said to each other remains unknown, but pious legends have sprung up around that meeting, according to which the "friar of the stigmata" predicted to the young priest of Cracow that he would one day become Pope and that an assassination attempt would be made against him.

When Wojtyla was auxiliary bishop of Cracow and on his way to Rome in 1962 for the Second Vatican Council, he was deeply concerned about a woman in his diocese whom he knew well. Wojtyla had first met Dr. Wanda Poltawska, a psychiatrist, in 1950 when he was a young priest. She had sought his help while caring for a pregnant, unmarried girl. A friendship had been formed, and a spiritual collaboration that has lasted ever since. Doctors had diagnosed Poltawska as having throat cancer and planned shortly to subject her to a desperate medical procedure.

The bishop's thoughts turned to the Italian friar, to whom many spiritual and corporeal wonders had been attributed. He dispatched a letter asking for Padre Pio's intervention: "Venerable Father, I ask that you pray for a forty-year-old mother of four girls, in Cracow, Poland (who during the

19

last war spent five years in a concentration camp), who is now in very grave danger related to her health and possibly may die because of cancer: that God may extend his mercy to this woman and her family in the presence of the Most Blessed Virgin. Most obligated in Christ, Karol Wojtyla."[1]

The messenger who carried the letter to Padre Pio was Angelo Battisti, the administrator of the House for the Relief of Suffering, a hospital built with the help of Padre Pio. Battisti provides us with the following personal testimony: "Having just arrived at the monastery, Padre Pio told me to read the letter to him. He listened to the brief message in Latin, then said: 'To this request one cannot say "no" ', and then added, 'Angelino, save this letter because one day it will become important'."[2]

Eleven days later, the reverend friar received a second letter from the bishop: "Venerable Father, the woman living in Cracow, Poland, mother of four young girls, on November 21, just before a surgical operation, suddenly recovered her health. Thanks be to God. Also to you, venerable Father, I give the greatest thanks in the name of the husband and all the family. In Christ, Karol Wojtyla."[3]

The hoped-for wonder had occurred. Yet it was understandable that Poltawska, because of her scientific training and rational temperament, was hesitant to believe that her sudden cure was attributable to the intervention of Padre Pio. At the same time, she was extremely grateful for her unexpected and complete recovery. Consequently, she decided

[1] The letter was written in Latin and reached Padre Pio on November 18, 1962.

[2] Tommaso Ricci, "And Thanks to Him Wojtyla Obtained the Miracle", 30 *Days*, December 1988, pp. 74–77.

[3] Ibid. The day after Karol Wojtyla was elected Pope, journalists found Padre Pio's *Letters* among Cardinal Wojtyla's Italian notebooks.

to travel to Pietrelcina, where the Capuchin friar resided. The two had never met before, but during his celebration of the Mass, Padre Pio paused momentarily and looked directly at the pilgrim from Poland, conveying to her the message that he knew she was the woman for whom he had prayed. This incident, together with others of an equally mystical nature, gave Poltawska the assurance she sought.[4]

Poltawska became director of the Marriage and Family Institute in Cracow, Poland, and an important adviser to Pope John Paul II on matters of marriage and the family. She went on to write the book *And I Am Afraid of My Dreams,*[5] which recounts her brutal internment at Ravensbrück from the time she was nineteen until she was twenty-three years of age. Her book expresses, according to one reviewer, moved by the stark contrast between her caring attitude and the utter lack of humanity she suffered at the hands of the Nazis, "the spark of human heroism, the light of humanity shining in the appalling darkness".[6]

Commentary

The inability to care, more than anything else, shows a human being to be inhuman. This is because caring for others is so fundamental to human nature as to coincide with it. To care is to express humanness. Not to care is to place a barrier between oneself and one's own humanity. The truest name for the human person, therefore, is "Care".

[4] From a personal meeting between Dr. Poltawska and the author, Toledo, Ohio, May 4–5, 1990.

[5] Wanda Poltawska, *And I Am Afraid of My Dreams,* trans. Mary Craig (New York: Hippocrene Books, 1989).

[6] James Sullivan, *Lay Witness,* vol. 11, no. 4 (December 1989): p. 13.

An ancient Roman myth personifies this notion in the following way: One day Care was amusing herself by molding earth into various shapes. She fashioned one shape that especially amused her. Wanting this new form to enjoy life, she beseeched Jupiter to grant it a soul. Jupiter obliged Care by breathing life into the earthly form. Care then requested that this new creature be named after her. When Jupiter objected, they asked Saturn, the god of Time, to serve as arbiter. Saturn decreed that when the new creature died, its body had to return to Earth, which was its origin; its soul had to return to its father, Jupiter, who had given it life. But all the Time it was alive it was to be entrusted to Care.[7]

Harvard scholar and poet Henry Wadsworth Longfellow, who had a great affection for the myths of antiquity, also wrote about the primal place of time and care in the constitution of man. He conceived an image that exquisitely parallels the Roman myth: "The every-day cares and duties, which men call drudgery, are the weights and counterpoises of the clock of time, giving its pendulum a true vibration, and its hands a regular motion; and when they cease to hang upon the wheels, the pendulum no longer swings, the hands no longer move, and the clock stands still." The absence of care is the death of personality. Care may seem to be a weight, but in fact it is the counterweight that gives life its balance, its vibrancy, its own authenticity.

Yet the central problem with care is precisely that many view it as drudgery. No doubt caring can be inconvenient upon occasion and can make considerable demands on our time. Indeed, the many cares of life can be exhausting. Shakespeare said that we needed sleep to knot up the rav-

---

[7] Martin Heidegger, *Being and Time,* trans. Macquarrie and Robinson (New York: Harper and Row, 1962), p. 242.

eled sleeve of care.[8] And Milton, in "L'Allegro", derided Care as a wrinkled old hag.[9] It is an irony at the core of the human personality that the caring that makes us authentic can appear so burdensome that a person can prefer to be other than who he is. Sluggishness, indifference to others, is therefore commonplace. Thus, Mother Teresa of Calcutta can say that "The greatest disease in the West is not tuberculosis or leprosy; it is being unwanted, unloved, and uncared for."[10]

In *"Terms of Endearment"*, a movie that won five Academy Awards, including "Best Picture", Emma, played by Debra Winger, gets a hefty dose of what it is like to be abandoned by her friends. At an afternoon luncheon, Emma excuses herself from the table. When she returns she finds an empty table. Her companions have deserted the restaurant like rats from a sinking ship, because one of them has disclosed the fact that Emma has cancer. Wounded and infuriated, Emma leaves the restaurant and catches up with her friend Patsy on the street. Emma tells Patsy that she cannot comprehend how people can be so self-absorbed and uncaring, how they can go through life with so little regard for the needs of others. Patsy, who is clearly embarrassed by the confrontation, asks, "What do you want me to tell them?"

"I don't mind them knowing [about the cancer]", Emma answers, referring to the other three who are now out of sight. "In less than two hours two of 'em told me they had had abortions. Three of them told me they were divorced. One of them hasn't talked to her mother in four years. And

[8] William Shakespeare, *Macbeth*, 2.2.43.

[9] John Milton, "L'Allegro", 1.31.

[10] Mother Teresa, *A Simple Path*, comp. Lucinda Vardey (New York: Ballantine Books, 1995), p. 79.

that one that has her little Natalie in a boarding school because she has to travel for her job? I mean help, Patsy, that's our ... Oh! the one with the yeast disease; she had vaginal herpes! If that's fit conversation for lunch, what's so God-awful terrible about my little tumors? I want you to tell them it ain't so tragic. People do get better. Tell them its okay to talk about the *cancer.*"

The word that Emma did not get out is probably "duty". It is our duty to care for others, not to avoid them, especially when they need us. But how, Emma must have wondered, can her friends breezily chat about each other's moral infirmities and remain utterly terrified of those of a medical nature? Perhaps they are afraid of the possibility that her suffering will impose unknown demands upon them. Perhaps they are also afraid to face death, not only hers but also their own. It escapes them that the death of the soul is more serious than the disintegration of the body.

The excuse is often given that people are too busy "being themselves" to be concerned about others. Henrik Ibsen's enduring character Peer Gynt travels to an insane asylum where the superintendent, Mr. Begriffenfeldt, tells him about people who are preoccupied with nothing more than themselves. "It's here that men are most themselves—themselves and nothing but themselves—sailing with outspread sails of self. Each shuts himself in a cask of self, the cask stopped with the bung of self and seasoned in a well of self. None has a tear for others' woes or cares what any other thinks."[11]

Wanda Poltawska, despite the horrifying ordeal she experienced at Ravensbrück, has never lost her caring concern for others. As a psychiatrist, she draws from her experience to

---

[11] Henrik Ibsen, *Peer Gynt* (New York: Airmont Publishing, 1967), p. 109.

provide specialized care to others who have suffered from the horrors of war and genocide.

When Karol Wojtyla, as Pope John Paul II, was shot in a failed assassination attempt, the first thing he did once released from the hospital was to visit his assailant in prison and pardon him. Even those who contest his words do not challenge his integrity and his care for others—including those who have trespassed against him.

Care does not allow suffering, either in the self or in the other, to prevent love from being expressed. It is the virtue that allows love to overcome its first and most fundamental obstacle, namely, inconvenience. In this regard, care is the one virtue that most closely resembles love.

CHASTITY

H IS GREAT UNCLE was the bearded terror Barbarossa. His second cousin was the brutal Emperor Frederick II of Germany, the infamous "Wonder of the World". His family was related to Emperor Henry VI and to the Kings of Aragon, Castile, and France, as well as to a good half of the ruling houses of Europe. His father rode in armor behind imperial banners and stormed the Benedictine monastery at Monte Cassino because the Emperor regarded it as a fortress of his enemy, the Pope. At his birth, therefore, this seventh and last son born to Count Landulf and his wife, the Countess Theodora of Teano,[1] inherited the clear and unbarterable obligation to take his place in the world and bring added luster to his family's already glorious name. His destiny was carved in stone. Or so it seemed.

When he calmly announced his intention to join a newly formed order of preachers and don the garb of a poor friar—a beggar, in fact—his family was both astonished and outraged. It were as if Napoleon had insisted on remaining a private soldier for the duration of his military career.[2] Anticipating the worst, he, with the master general of the order and three other friars, set out on foot to leave Rome

[1] Jacques Maritain, *St. Thomas Aquinas,* trans. J. Evans and P. O'Reilly (New York: Meridian Books, 1965), p. 25.

[2] G. K. Chesterton, *Saint Thomas Aquinas,* in *The Collected Works of G. K. Chesterton,* vol. 2 (San Francisco: Ignatius Press, 1986), p. 451.

and escape to Paris. His mother dispatched a message to two of her sons who were soldiers in the army of Frederick II. She ordered them to kidnap her fugitive offspring. The brothers did as they were commanded, forcibly apprehended the black sheep of their clan, and imprisoned him at the fortress of Monte San Giovanni, near his birthplace in Roccasecca.[3]

During his eighteen-month period of incarceration, every means, fair and foul, was used to shake him from his resolve to become a Dominican preacher. Members of his family took turns in resorting to a wide assortment of strategies: kindness and harsh treatment, blandishments and threats, deprivation of food and books. His eldest sister, Marotta, who was sent to convert him, was herself converted by him and joined the order of Saint Benedict. The family's patience must have been at the point of exhaustion when his brother Raynaldo adopted a more forthright and devilish plan of luring him from his purpose.[4]

Raynaldo was an upright and honorable man in the eyes of the world, but he lived and thought in accordance with the world. He introduced into the room where his youngest brother was sleeping a woman who has been described as a "courtesan of the most exclusive sort",[5] a "pretty young girl, with all the charms of the temptress".[6]

The young friar at the time was a full-blooded man of about nineteen years of age. He was a strong and healthy

[3] Martin Grabmann, *Thomas Aquinas,* trans. Virgil Michel (Toronto: Longmans, Green, 1928), p. 2.

[4] Gerald Vann, *Saint Thomas Aquinas* (New York: Benziger Brothers, 1947), p. 43.

[5] Reginald Coffey, "St. Thomas Aquinas", in Thomas Aquinas, *Summa Theologiae* (New York: Benziger Brothers, 1948), 3:3,064.

[6] Maritain, op. cit., p. 30.

individual of impressive stature. No doubt he had learned, along with his brothers, how to mount and ride a horse and to execute other manly arts expected of men of nobility growing up in thirteenth century Italy. His long period of confinement and deprivation must have left him vulnerable to enticements of the flesh. Upon seeing the woman and immediately sizing up her purpose, he grabbed hold of a flaming firebrand, chased her out of the cell, and traced the sign of the cross on the door with the brand.[7] He was in no mood to reason with her. "Then", according to one commentator, "he returned, and dropped it [the firebrand] again into the fire; and sat down on that seat of sedentary scholarship, that chair of philosophy, that secret throne of contemplation, from which he never rose again."[8]

His family may have been convinced that their prisoner was incorrigible. They may have feared the wrath of Pope Innocent IV, who, by that time, had been alerted to the travesty that was taking place. Or his mother may have experienced a change of heart. For whatever reason, he was soon permitted to escape. He was lowered in a basket and received into the arms of joyful Dominicans. In the company of his fellow friars, he then set out for Paris, arriving without further interruption.

Neither his lineage nor the atmosphere that surrounded his arrival in the world could have augured his career as a white knight of God, a staunch champion of the spirit in its war against the flesh. Before he was born, however, a holy hermit is reported to have foretold his career, saying to his mother, Theodora: "He will enter the Order of Friars Preachers, and so great will be his learning and sanctity that

[7] Ibid.
[8] Chesterton, p. 454.

in his day no one will be found to equal him."[9] It is ironic that one of the doctrines he propounded is that grace is a more important factor than either heredity or environment.

Toward the end of his life, in his late forties, he confided to his faithful friend and companion Reginald of Piperno the secret of a remarkable gift he had received that allowed him to do his work without ever experiencing the slightest disturbance of the flesh. After he had driven the temptress from his chamber, he earnestly implored God to grant him integrity of mind and body. His prayer was answered, and the gift bestowed upon him was made apparent to those who call him the "Angelic Doctor".

His intellectual contribution was immense, involving an unprecedented synthesis between philosophy and theology, pagan thought and Christian faith, and the contributions of antiquity and the insights of the contemporary world. Because of this, Pope Leo XIII could say of him: "Among the Scholastic Doctors, the chief and master of all, towers Thomas Aquinas, who, as Cajetan observes, because 'he most venerated the ancient doctors of the Church, in a certain way seems to have inherited the intellect of all.' "[10]

Commentary

Chastity is the virtue that brings the sexual appetite into harmony with reason. It requires, not the renunciation of sexuality, but the right or reasonable use of it. There are times when human beings should abstain from sexual pleasure,

[9] The prophecy is recorded by Peter Calo (1300), a biographer of Aquinas. See *The Catholic Encyclopedia,* ed. Herbermann et al. (New York: Robert Appleton, 1912), 14:663.
[10] Pope Leo XIII, *Aeterni Patris,* sec. 17.

but it is not necessary to abstain from activities that are conducted in accord with reason. By reason, we are referring, not to an abstract and impersonal set of rules separated from life, but the capacity to be realistic. Reason is a light that illuminates what we are doing so that we can behave in a way that is consistent with our best interest.

One of the fundamental problems that unchastity brings about is a blindness that leads directly to acts of imprudence. A person who is inflamed by lustful desires is hardly in a position to do what is good for himself or anyone else. It is well known that prostitutes can operate very effectively as spies by first seducing their man and then educing from him the valuable information he possesses. The intemperate military leader Holofernes literally lost his head because of his lust for Judith: "Her sandal ravished his eyes, her beauty took his soul captive, . . . and her sword cut off his head."[11]

Unchastity tends to destroy prudence and to prevent a person from maintaining the self-possession or integrity he needs in order to "be himself" in the proper sense of the term. In the absence of chastity, a person is easily seduced into doing things that are beneath his dignity, things that are shameful, things that do not accord with who he truly is. In writing about how unchastity corrupts prudence, the Thomist philosopher Josef Pieper writes: "Unchaste abandon and the self-surrender of the soul to the world of sensuality paralyzes the primordial powers of the moral person: the ability to perceive in silence the call of reality and to make, in the retreat of this silence, the decision appropriate to the concrete situation of concrete action."[12]

Aquinas acted prudently in chasing the prostitute away.

[11] Judith 16:9.
[12] Joseph Pieper, "Chastity and Unchastity", in *The Four Cardinal Virtues* (New York: Harcourt, Brace and World, 1965), p. 160.

Had he succumbed to her enticements, he may very well, in addition to breaking a commandment of God, have forfeited the serenity he needed in order to achieve the status of preeminence as a philosopher and theologian. No doubt he had a premonition of what was at stake. Aquinas' treatises on chastity indicate how clearly he saw the harm that unchastity posed for the moral and intellectual life. He lists the eight daughters of unchastity (or lust) as blindness of mind, rashness, thoughtlessness, inconstancy, inordinate self-love, hatred of God, excessive love of this world, and abhorrence or despair of a future world.[13] He explains that they wreak havoc with the four acts of reason and the twofold orientation of the will. Blindness hinders one's ability to apprehend an object rightly. Rashness interferes with counsel. Thoughtlessness opposes judgment about what is to be done. And inconstancy conflicts with reason's command about what is to be done. Inordinate self-love is contrary to the will's proper end, which is God, while hatred of God flows from his forbidding acts of lust. Love of this world is inimical to the means man should will in relation to his end, while despair of a future world results from the distaste of spiritual pleasures brought on by over-indulgence in the pleasures of the flesh.

Unchastity can be ruinous of a personality. In Shakespeare's *Measure for Measure,* Angelo offers to spare the life of Isabella's brother, Claudio, who faces death because of sexual misconduct, if she consents to sleep with him. When Isabella, who is a novice in a cloistered order of nuns, discusses the matter with her brother, she is horrified to discover what a despicable rake he has become as a result of his carnal misadventures. "Death is a fearful thing", says Claudio, who has little

---

[13] Thomas Aquinas, *Summa Theologiae,* II–II, 153, 5.

regard for his sister's chastity. "And shamed life a hateful", replies Isabella. Claudio becomes more earnest in his plea: "Sweet sister, let me live: What sin you do to save a brother's life, / Nature dispenses with the deed so far / That it becomes a virtue." Her response is most emphatic:

> O you beast!
> O faithless coward! O dishonest wretch!
> Wilt thou be made a man out of my vice?
> Is't not a kind of incest, to take life
> From thine own sister's shame?

She breaks off any further discussion by exclaiming that for Claudio, fornication was not a lapse but a life-style: "Thy sin's not accidental, but a trade, / Mercy to thee would prove itself a bawd: / 'Tis best that thou diest quickly."[14] Claudio's preoccupation with sexual pleasure, which had become a "trade", or a cold-blooded way of life, poisoned his soul to the degree that his own sister's honor meant nothing to him. In fact, poor Claudio had lost all sense of right and wrong. He loved his own life inordinately and to the exclusion of all else. Lust had taken possession of him.

Chastity is a most honorable virtue. It honors the self as well as the other. It may be a difficult virtue to attain, not because sexual desire is so intense, but because it is constantly being aroused when society can think of little else. Friedrich Nietzsche, no friend of Christianity, recognized the validity of this point. In *Thus Spake Zarathustra,* he begins his chapter "Of Chastity" by stating, "I love the forest. It is bad to live in towns: too many of the lustful live there."[15] Aquinas, long before there were mass media,

[14] William Shakespeare, *Measure for Measure,* 3.1.

[15] Friedrich Nietzsche, *Thus Spoke Zarathustra,* trans. R. J. Hollingdale (Harmondsworth, Middlesex, Eng.: Penguin Books, 1969), p. 81.

understood only too well the dangerous role environmental seduction could play: "There is not much sinning because of natural desires.... But the stimuli of desire which man's cunning has devised are something else, and for the sake of these sins one sins very much."[16]

---

[16] Pieper, loc. cit., p. 173.

COMPASSION

PERHAPS NO OTHER intellectual in the history of Western thought defies categorization more thoroughly than Simone Weil. She was born into a Jewish household but cultivated an ardent love for Catholicism. She fell in love with Saint Francis, it is said, as soon as she heard of him and fell to her knees in awe when she visited the Poverello's chapel in Assisi.[1] Yet she never entered the Church, believing that it was God's will that she not become a Catholic. By quoting passages of Racine by heart at six years of age she already showed signs of the intellectual prowess that would characterize her adult life. She taught philosophy at several schools, intermittently, between the menial jobs she took in order to gain a deeper personal understanding of the working class. Although her thinking was decidedly left of center, and she made a regular practice of picketing factories and disseminating leftist literature, she deplored any form of socialism. She was a social philosopher and a mystic, a Christian and a Jew, a European and a student of Hindu thought and the Sanskrit language. She was an enigma; but she is remembered.

The common thread that gave the seemingly disparate aspects of her life a certain constancy was her profound compassion for the afflicted, a compassion that literally

[1] Vernon Sproxton, "Pilgrim of the Absolute", in *Gateway to God,* ed. David Raper (New York: Crossroad, 1982), p. 23.

verged on identification. All gaps that separated human beings from each other were a lifelong concern for Weil. She wanted these gaps to be filled with love. "All sins", she once wrote, "are attempts to fill voids."[2] Simone de Beauvoir said of her, "Her heart would miss a beat for something that happened at the other end of the earth."[3]

Weil's powerful identification with the deprived was foreshadowed when she was a child. At the age of five she refused to eat sugar because French soldiers at the front during World War I had none. In her mid-twenties she took a year's leave of absence from teaching and worked at the Renault automobile factory so she could experience the psychological effects of heavy industrial labor. An attack of pleurisy, however, forced her to abandon the job, and she returned to her teaching post. Later, despite her continuing poor health, she became a cook on the Catalonian front during the Spanish Civil War and suffered the complete invasion of her inner life by the horror of war. When she worked in England with the French Resistance, its leader thwarted her desire to be parachuted into occupied France. She refused to take any more food than the small rations her French compatriots were given under German occupation, because she wanted to share the hardships of those she had left in France. Her malnutrition, together with a number of other ailments, brought about her death in 1943 at age thirty-four.

Weil has been praised and criticized: praised for her humane compassion, criticized for her presumed foolishness. "She

[2] Simone Weil, *La Pesanteur et la grace* (Paris: Plon Collectiom L'épi, 1947), p. 27: "Tous les Péchés sont de tentatives pour combler des vides."

[3] Sproxton, loc. cit., p. 17.

was a fanatic in search of a fanaticism", states one critic.[4] Some saw her as a modern saint; others denounced her policy of social action as one rich in good intentions but poor in practical results. Her varied critics are a logical extension of her varied life. But the judgment one might have concerning the life of Simone Weil ought not to obscure appreciation of her thought, particularly in reference to what she had to say about compassion.

What emerges from the writings of Simone Weil is the clear notion that the fundamental relationship between human beings should be one of love and that love is the factor that orchestrates virtue. According to Weil, the practice of separating justice from love, for example, contradicts the gospel, which makes no distinction between the two. The person who is just but not loving may fulfill his obligations, and his beneficiaries may express servile thanks, but a cold alienation remains nonetheless. In order to overcome the alienation that separates people, virtues must be administered through love and returned through love. She writes: "Only the absolute identification of justice and love make the co-existence possible of compassion and gratitude on the one hand, and on the other, of respect for the dignity of affliction in the afflicted—respect felt by the sufferer himself and the others."[5]

Love, for Weil, obliterates distances and inequalities. In the absence of love, these gaps endure. The gap between the powerful and the weak, the healthy and the sick, can be overcome by loving compassion. Through compassion, love identifies with those who are afflicted; through generosity,

[4] George Will, *The Pursuit of Happiness and Other Sobering Thoughts* (New York: Harper Colophon, 1978), p. 17.
[5] Simone Weil, *Waiting on God,* trans. Emma Craufurd (Glasgow, Scotland: William Collins, 1950), p. 97.

love gives of itself to them. The model for this unification of love and virtue, for Weil, is Christ: "Generosity and compassion are inseparable, and both have their model in God, that is to say in creation and in the Passion."[6] Here, Weil is on firm Christian ground. Saint Bernard was saying something quite similar in the twelfth century: "For just as pure truth is seen only with a pure heart, so a brother's misery is truly felt with a miserable heart. But in order to have a miserable heart because of another's misery, you must first know your own; so that you may find your neighbor's mind in your own and know from yourself how to help him, by the example of our Savior, who willed his passion in order to learn compassion; his misery, to learn commiseration."[7]

Weil's thoughts concerning love and virtue are tightly integrated with God. Only the unity between God, love, and virtue can overcome the separation between men brought about by matter, power, and affliction: "In true love it is not we who love the afflicted in God; it is God in us who loves them. . . . Compassion and gratitude come down from God, and when they are exchanged in a glance, God is present at the point where the edges of those who give and those who receive meet."[8]

Weil's social philosophy may not have produced much social reform. But her thoughts concerning compassion are humane, noble, and sound. They offer a world that is reeling from alienation, at the very least, a beautiful image of that loving glance where neighbor meets neighbor in God's embrace.

An anonymous donor has attached a small plaque to the simple stone that marks Weil's grave. The words inscribed

---

[6] Ibid., p. 103.
[7] Bernard, *The Steps of Humility*, 3.
[8] Weil, *Waiting*, p. 107.

are Italian: "La mia solitudine l'altrui dolore germivo fino all
morte [My solitude held in its grasp the grief of others till
my death]."[9] Although the author of this phrase remains
unknown, the sentiment perfectly captures the life and spirit
of the enigma that is Simone Weil.

Commentary

Whereas chastity is the contemporary world's most unpopu-
lar virtue, compassion is clearly its favorite. It has become a
cultural imperative that we have compassion for others.
Compassion's popularity, unfortunately, is so great that it
tends to isolate this virtue from all those other factors it
needs in order to remain truly a virtue. Consequently,
compassion becomes an argument unto itself, so to speak, to
justify abortion, sterilization, euthanasia, and sundry other
actions that are aimed at reducing the amount of misery that
currently afflicts mankind. Separated from love, light,
generosity, hope, patience, courage, and determination,
"compassion" becomes nothing more than a code word
whose real name is expediency. It may be true that more
lives are dispatched in the name of compassion than are lost
in wars. When compassion becomes a principle, it ceases to
be a virtue. As a principle, all it means is the easiest way out.

Back in 1987, the Tower Commission, which investigated
the arms-to-Iran operation that transpired during the Reagan
administration, reported that the President was motivated
to sell arms to the Iranian regime of Ayatollah Khomeini by
the "compassion" he had for Americans held hostage in
Lebanon. As the report stated: "It was this intense compas-

[9] Sproxton, loc. cit., p. 28.

sion for the hostages that appeared to motivate his steadfast support of the Iran initiative, even in the face of opposition from his secretaries of state and defense."[10]

Like our civic leaders, our celebrities boast about how compassionate they are. They seem always to be looking for the next group on whom to exercise their compassion—the homeless, the farmers, those with AIDS. But the more enthusiasm there is for compassion, the less there is for justice. We are so compassionate toward criminals that we shudder to think of punishing them. Such superinflated compassion not only crowds out justice, it crowds out common sense.

The person who possesses true fraternal compassion would prefer to find nothing in others that would elicit his compassion, but if he did find something, he would then need to exercise other virtues in order to have the power to respond properly. Compassion helps us to identify with the sufferings of others, but it does not of itself provide us with a key as to what we should do. "The dew of compassion is a tear", as Lord Byron said, but the "do" of compassion is "unclear". Poor Hamlet had plenty of compassion for the suffering soul of his betrayed and murdered father, but he lacked the prudence, the courage, and the justice to "do the right thing".

Saint Thomas Aquinas discusses the virtue of *compassio* in his *Summa Theologiae* where he responds to a somewhat curious question: "Whether pain and sorrow are assuaged by the compassion of friends?"[11] The question may seem curious to the modern mind because the answer seems to be

---

[10] "Arms Probe Faults Reagan, Key Advisers", AP, Kitchener-Waterloo *Record,* February 26, 1987, p. A–1.

[11] Thomas Aquinas, *Summa Theologiae*, I–II, 38, 3: "Utrum dolor et tristitia mitigentur per compassionem amicorum?"

evident. Aquinas' reasoning, however, is most illuminating. He offers two reasons for his affirmative answer. The first is that compassionate friends are able to share and therefore lighten another's burden. Pain and sorrow have a depressing effect, not unlike that of a weight from which we want to be freed. When we are greeted by compassionate friends, we sense that they are bearing our burden with us, striving, as it were, to lessen its weight. As a result, our burden becomes easier to bear. The second reason he presents is, in his opinion, better than the first because it is more positive. He argues that because the virtue of compassion is rooted in love, when a person who is suffering witnesses the love his friends have for him, he experiences a pleasure that assuages his sorrow and mitigates his pain.

Aquinas did not write about compassion as extensively or as often as did Arthur Schopenhauer, who is more identified with it than is any other philosopher. Schopenhauer, also the most pessimistic of all philosophers, found man to be such a "grotesque caricature"[12] and his lot so hopelessly miserable that "compassion" becomes the one virtue whose need towers above all the rest. His compassion is heavily tinged with pity because he sees death as the only redemption for the crime of being born.[13] For Aquinas, compassion is lived with hope because it is inseparable from love, and it is through love that man is to be redeemed. The contemporary and immensely popular view of compassion bears a stronger resemblance to that of Schopenhauer than to that of Saint Thomas, for, according to its logic, compassion should remove suffering by removing the sufferer. It is

[12] Arthur Schopenhauer, "On the Suffering of the World", in *The Meaning of Life,* ed. S. Sanders and D. Cheney (Englewood Cliffs, N.J.: Prentice-Hall, 1980), p. 31.

[13] Ibid., p. 32.

of course easier to solve the problem of suffering this way. But ease is no friend of virtue and therefore of little real help to the sufferer.

COURAGE

JUST A YEAR before her death in 1963, she sang from the top of the Eiffel Tower, on an enormous platform that overlooked the entire city of Paris. The man who introduced her that night, Joseph Kessel, had been present when she sang in a nightclub for the first time. He recalled her ravaged face and the ragged sweater she had worn, which bore eloquent testimony to the suffering of her childhood. He spoke of her voice, which was already filled with the "unique genius that moved us so in the following years". He paid tribute to the "incredible courage" she exemplified in overcoming poverty, weakness, and anguish, and the discipline she showed in achieving artistic standards of the highest order.[1] At her public funeral the following year, everyone in Paris seemed to throng the streets to get a final glimpse of their beloved *chanteuse*.

She was born into abject poverty as Edith Giovanna Gassion on December 19, 1915. She was named in honor of Edith Cavell,[2] the courageous British nurse who had been

---

[1] Monique Lange, *Piaf*, trans. Richard Woodward (New York: Seaver Books, 1981), p. 250.

[2] Edith Cavell was in charge of a hospital in Brussels, Belgium, when German troops occupied the city. She assisted Allied soldiers, about two hundred in all, in escaping to the Dutch border. She was arrested and executed before a German firing squad. "Patriotism is not enough" were her last words. Mount Edith Cavell in Jasper National Park, Alberta, Canada, is named after her.

killed by a German firing squad just a few days earlier for helping Allied soldiers to escape. Her mother, a prostitute, abandoned Gassion in infancy. Her maternal grandmother took care of her initially, but when her father came home on leave from the war and found his two-year-old daughter in such deplorable health, he spirited her away to live with his own mother, who worked as a cook in a "house of a rather special sort".[3]

At the age of three, Gassion suddenly became blind. Her condition may have been an inflammation of the cornea, known as keratitis, which the body is able to ward off on its own. Nonetheless, the "ladies" of the house—her "multiple mothers", so to speak—believed that her recovery was brought about through the intercession of Saint Thérèse of Lisieux. They had taken little Edith to the nearby town of Lisieux and together prayed for a miracle. Ten days later, at four o'clock in the afternoon, she could see again. The women closed their house the next Sunday and returned to Lisieux to give thanks to the "Little Flower". Gassion herself always believed her cure was miraculous. According to her own testimony, she never failed to carry with her the image of Saint Thérèse.[4]

The name by which the world knew her was Piaf, a French slang word for "sparrow", chosen by the cabaret owner who gave Gassion her first break as a singer. She was, indeed, like a sparrow, standing no more than four feet ten inches and weighing a mere ninety pounds. Though small in stature, she was able to bear tremendous burdens. When the man who launched her singing career was brutally murdered by thieves, she was arrested and charged as the

[3] Lange, *Piaf,* p. 17.
[4] Edith Piaf, *The Wheel of Fortune,* trans. P. Trewartha and A. de Virton (Bath, Eng.: Chivers Press, 1965), p. 132.

prime suspect in the case. When Edith was nineteen, the only child she would ever have died of meningitis. One of her many lovers, the world champion middle-weight boxer Marcel Cerdan, died in an airplane crash. Gassion suffered through three automobile accidents, several operations, and various illnesses. Though her life was one of almost unremitting suffering and disappointment, she could think of others. She sang for French prisoners of war during World War II and, like the heroine for whom she was named, aided several in their escape.

She had the extraordinary ability to transmute her pain through her music, bringing hope and inspiration to her millions of listeners. She put her entire being into her singing. The celebrated poet and playwright Jean Cocteau said of her: "Every time she sings you have the feeling she's wrenching her soul from her body for the last time."[5] This may have been most evident when she performed the songs she herself had composed, such as the immensely popular "La Vie en Rose". Cocteau also once said, "If Piaf dies, part of me will die with her." Ironically, he and Gassion died on the same day.[6]

In her final months, she dictated her memoirs from a hospital bed. They were published shortly after her death under the title *My Life*. Looking back on her life, she singled out the important role courage played in her struggles. "It's true that I've always wanted to have courage", she wrote. "They say that it's a masculine quality. But I believe that it's women who 'cope' best when things are going badly. It's a question of habit, especially for me. My apprenticeship in life was not particularly rosy."[7]

[5] Lange, *Piaf,* p. 23.

[6] Ibid., p. 250.

[7] Edith Piaf, *My Life,* trans. Margaret Crossland (London: Peter Owen, 1990), p. 97.

Her final memoirs are also a confession. Not wanting to ignore her faults, she expressed the hope that it might be said of her what was said of Mary Magdalen: "Her many sins are forgiven, for she loved much."[8]

The life of Edith Piaf demonstrates the irrepressibility of the human spirit: it can flower in the most unpromising places. As G. K. Chesterton once remarked: "If seeds in the black earth can turn into such beautiful roses, what might not the heart of man become in its long journey toward the stars."

Commentary

Courage is not the same as fearlessness. It is not the absence of fear but the control of it; "grace under pressure", as Ernest Hemingway said. Fear, if left unchecked, sweeps over a person and renders him incapable of responding intelligently and effectively to a difficult situation. Fear concentrates on what can go wrong and in so doing interferes with one's confidence in being able to execute what is right. Martin Luther King, Jr., spoke of the need for building "dykes of courage to hold back the flood of fear". Courage gets above fear; it is, so to speak, fear that has said its prayers.

We tend to think of courage in militaristic terms as a heroic stance against exceptionally fearsome and life-threatening adversaries. We think of Horatio at the Bridge, James Bowie at the Alamo, or World War I flying ace Eddie Rickenbacker gunning down twenty-two enemy planes.

[8] Ibid., p. 10.

These men were surely courageous. And theirs is the courage that makes one's heart stop. But courage is not restricted to daring military accomplishments.

Emily Dickinson, the diminutive poet-recluse known as the "Belle of Amherst", never had an opportunity to develop the courage a soldier needs on the battlefield. She fought only the enemies of the soul and had to find perhaps an even stronger courage to face them: "To fight aloud is very brave, / But gallanter, I know, / Who charge within the bosom / The cavalry of woe."[9]

That interior cavalry can be a formidable adversary requiring no end of courage. Anxiety, doubts, disappointments, uncertainties, and the like, because they are not as sharply drawn or clearly seen as external enemies, pose a difficult challenge. The "dark night of the soul" demands a degree of courage that one should not underestimate. "O the mind, mind has mountains", wrote Gerard Manley Hopkins, "cliffs of fall / Frightful, sheer, no-man-fathomed. Hold them cheap / May who ne'er hung there."[10]

Robert Louis Stevenson is one of the most admired personalities in the history of English literature largely because of the courage he expressed in working diligently and uncomplainingly in the face of great difficulties, especially the poor health that plagued him all his life. Though he filled his books with exciting characters and exotic places, he was more interested in man's inner spirit. He held that everyone needed to possess courage, even those who outwardly lived less than adventurous lives. He said that the ordinary person is no less noble because no drum beats

[9] Emily Dickinson, *First Series, Life,* XVI, stanza 1.

[10] W. H. Gardiner, ed., "No Worst There Is None", in *Gerard Manley Hopkins: A Selection of His Poems and Prose* (London: Penguin Books, 1953), p. 61.

before him when he goes out to his daily battlefields and no crowds shout his arrival when he returns from his encounter with victory and defeat.

Courage is not something we need rarely but what we need on a daily basis. We all need courage to live, suffer, struggle, and die. In fact, say the existentialist philosophers, we need courage "to be". Winston Churchill ranked courage as "the first of human qualities because it is the quality which guarantees all the others". The scholastics referred to courage as "fortitude" and defined it in very broad terms as the virtue that enables us to face firmly and undismayed the difficulties and dangers that stand in the way of duty and goodness.[11]

In the Pulitzer Prize winning study of political fortitude, *Profiles in Courage,* John F. Kennedy argued that the opportunities to be courageous are presented to all of us. "To be courageous", he wrote, "requires no exceptional qualifications, no magic formula, no special combination of time, place and circumstance."[12] We are all obliged to find courage in our day-to-day existence in order to resist the temptation to sacrifice our integrity for the promise of an easier life. Courage allows us to maintain our personal authenticity at times when surrendering to the familiar and the secure is most inviting. The famed aviatrix Amelia Earhart understood that without courage, personal contentment is not possible. "Courage is the price that life extracts for granting peace", she wrote. "The soul that knows it not, knows no release from little things."

Our birth is a release from a world where everything we

[11] Fulton J. Sheen, *The Seven Virtues* (New York: P. J. Kennedy and Sons, 1940), p. 4.

[12] John F. Kennedy, *Profiles in Courage* (New York: Harper and Row, 1964), p. 266.

need is systematically provided for us. Each step in the process of becoming a mature person requires birth pangs of one sort or another. We cannot reach for the stars unless we first release ourselves from what holds us back. Courage is both an emancipation as well as an adventure.

COURTESY

T HE TERM "courtesy" derives from the word "court". A courteous person, according to the etymology, behaves in a manner befitting a prince. Courtly love is a romanticized version of sexual love that originated among the French aristocracy in the late eleventh century but soon spread into neighboring countries through the poetry and music of itinerant romantics called "troubadours". Manuals called "courtesy books" circulated to advise aspiring young courtiers in etiquette and other aspects of behavior expected at royal or noble courts. They helped to elevate courtship—the implementation of courtly love—to a highly refined art.

At the same time, there were certain ambiguities about courtly love, as specific cognates of the word "courtesy" clearly attest. A courtesan, that is, a woman attached to the court, is a prostitute; but a curtsy—the word "courtesy" reduced to two syllables—was an elegant gesture of respect. Courtly love in all its aspects is dramatized in the legends of King Arthur and his knights of the Round Table. Sir Lancelot's tragic love for Lady Guinevere is the archetypal embodiment of this form of romantic desire, in which the woman is greatly idealized and ardently pursued. But as in the case of Lancelot and Guinevere, one of the less respectable features of courtly love, given the prevalent medieval practice of marriage for convenience, was the rationalization of adultery.[1]

Saint Francis of Assisi was greatly enamored by the ideal of courtly love and the songs of the troubadours, and he gave them a Christian interpretation.[2] He took the courtly notion of courtesy and gave it a fresh countenance that glowed with Christian charity. For Francis, courtesy became the respect one was prepared to show in the presence of anyone. He was especially fond of expressing this virtue to the less fortunate members of society. For Francis, the poor, the sick, and the neglected were his "brothers". "Whoever may come to us," he said to his disciples, "whether a friend or a foe, a thief or a robber, let him be kindly received."[3] He knighted all humanity and then, with an almost reckless enthusiasm, began addressing all God's creatures with the honorific titles of "brother" and "sister". He praised Brother Sun and Sister Moon, Brother Wind and Sister Water. According to the legend, his "little brethren the birds" listened so devoutly to his sermon by the roadside near Bevagna that he chided himself for not having thought of preaching to them before. The special Lady this gallant and exuberant troubadour chose to court was Lady Poverty. He pursued his Lady ardently throughout his life and, when he was dying, requested that his body be stripped naked, laid on the bare earth and sprinkled with ashes as a sign that even in death he had remained faithful to her.

Francis was courteous to all of God's creatures because

[1] C. S. Lewis, "Courtly Love", in *The Allegory of Love* (London: Oxford University Press, 1959).

[2] Seamus Mulholland, "St. Francis and the Themes of Medieval Literature", *The Cord: A Franciscan Spiritual Review,* April 1994, p. 117.

[3] *The Catholic Encyclopedia,* ed. C. G. Herbermann et al. (New York: Appleton, 1909), 6:227.

courtesy, in his view, was the younger sister of charity and an attribute of God. "La Cortesia e una delle proprieta di Dio [Courtesy is one of the attributes of God]", for "God Himself, of His courtesy, gives His sun and rain to the just and the unjust."[4] Francis would surely have applauded what Hilaire Belloc was later to say about courtesy:

> Of Courtesy, it is much less
> Than courage of heart or holiness,
> Yet in my walks it seems to me
> That the grace of God is Courtesy.[5]

Francis took the straitened notion of courtesy as sung by the troubadours and gave it a breadth that made it coextensive with the cosmos. He understood that royalty was not limited to aristocracy; it was an essential feature of every thing willed and loved into being by the King of Kings. All of creation stood before his eyes as one vast Royal Court. He had taken the word "court", which in Latin originally referred to something closed (*cors,* accusative *cortem:* an enclosure for cattle) and opened it up to the far reaches of the universe.

For Francis, courtesy is the glad tribute each pays to each in recognizing the likeness of God in every soul. It is the light of God that confers upon his human subjects a nobility that is radically different from the nobility that members of the court believed they saw in each other. It is not blood, rank, privilege, or even virtue that makes men noble; it is their Creator. Francis restored the source of nobility and the justification for courtesy to God, who himself is bound by courtesy to all souls who bear his image.

---

[4] Ibid.
[5] Hilaire Belloc, "Courtesy".

Francis had a rich appreciation for the virtue of courtesy understood in its highest form. Goethe indicates a similar appreciation when he writes: "There is no outward sign of true courtesy that does not rest on a deep moral foundation. . . . There is a courtesy of the heart; it is allied to love. From it springs the purest courtesy in the outward behavior." Likewise, Michel de Montaigne grasped its great value, not only in itself but for what it can produce: "Courtesy is a science of the highest importance. It is like grace and beauty in the body, which charm at first sight, and lead on to further intimacy and friendship."

Even the small kindnesses and seemingly trivial considerations that are shown to others can lend a greater charm to one's character than the display of great talents and accomplishments. They can provide the gateway to firm and enduring friendships, and they can also provide the world with much needed warmth and wit. During one of his performances, pianist-comedian Victor Borge was handed a note that read: "Lauritz Melchior and Jean Hersholt both at ringside." Borge responded with diplomacy and charm. "I rarely introduce big names from the stage," he said to his audience, "but in this case, since both visitors are old friends and fellow Danish Americans, I made an exception. I have the privilege of introducing two great Danish artists. I honestly don't know in what order to introduce them," he said, fearing that he might be discourteous to one or the other, "so I'm sure that Jean Hersholt won't mind if I mention Lauritz Melchior first."[6]

[6] "Eating Out", *The Bedside Book of Laughter* (London: Hazell Watson and Viney, 1959), p. 99.

Our contemporary world, however, so impressed as it is by the mere external show of things, has trivialized courtesy, transforming it into a tool of commerce. Thus, we write courtesy notes, make courtesy visits, present courtesy baskets, pick up courtesy tickets, and switch on courtesy lights in ways that may not reflect genuine courtesy. We use courtesy phones, report to courtesy desks, study courtesy maps, receive courtesy titles, and we are given the courtesy treatment to insure that we remain satisfied and steady customers. The courtesy industry is alive and well. Emerson, who once said, "Life is not so short but that there is always time for courtesy", might be appalled if he could observe the superficial ways in which we spend our current courtesy time.

Just as a halo does not have far to slip in order to become a noose, courtesy — like any other virtue — does not have far to stray to become a vice. Courtesy can easily be nothing more than a shallow pretense, a vulgar display of hypocrisy. As Shakespeare writes:

> How courtesy would seem to cover sin,
> When what is done is like an hypocrite,
> The which is good in nothing but in sight![7]

Courtesy is a true virtue only when it has a personal depth that accompanies its outward show. One might find genuine courtesy in the most unlikely places, far from either the court of ancient kings or the world of modern commerce:

> Shepherd, I take thy word,
> And trust thy honest-offered courtesy,
> Which oft is sooner found in lowly sheds

---

[7] William Shakespeare, *Pericles,* 1.1.121.

With smoky rafters, than in tap'stry halls
And courts of princes.[8]

Courtesy is paradoxical but immensely practical. The courteous person assumes that every man is a gentleman and every woman a lady and treats them accordingly. In doing so, a person displays the mark of a gentleman or a lady. It may seem to be naïve and gratuitous to make such an assumption, but it is remarkable how many people begin to act as gentlemen and as ladies simply because they were thought to be worthy of respect.

The foundation for courtesy is the dignity of man. Courtesy is the appropriate response to recognizing the divine imprint in another person. Graciousness, as its etymology indicates, is the "release of loveliness", a quality that emanates from the person who is being gracious. Courtesy is the recognition of that quality in others. In this regard, courtesy is something like love at first sight. It is sensing nobility at first sight and then acting in a manner consistent with that sense.

For Dante, this nobility is luminously evident to the souls in Paradise. In his "Paradiso" two Dominicans—Dominic and Aquinas—exchange courteous and joyful tributes with two Franciscans—Francis and Bonaventure. Aquinas first praises Francis for his great love for Lady Poverty:

And unto her he pledged his wedded faith
In spiritual court and before his father too,
And loved her more each day that he drew breath.[9]

---

[8] John Milton, *Comus* (1637), l. 321.

[9] Dante Alighieri, "Paradiso", *The Divine Comedy,* trans. Dorothy Sayers, II.I.61: "E dinanzi all sua spirital corte / e coram patre le si fece unito; / poscia di di in di l'amo più forte."

Bonaventure then extols Dominic as a great champion ("paladin") and acknowledges that he as well as his company of saints are very much moved by the words of Saint Thomas:

> To emulous praise of that great paladin,
> The modest speech and glowing courtesy
> Of Brother Thomas moved me, and therein
> Moved all this fellowship to join with me.[10]

The courtesy that these saints display toward each other represents the gracious mutuality and harmony that exists between souls in Paradise. Courtesy is of divine origin and is shared by all who participate in God's light.[11] The implication is apparent: we begin to experience what heaven must be like when we sense in each other our divine nobility and respond with the proper courtesy.

---

[10] Ibid., 12.1.143: "Ad inveggiar cotanto paladino / mi mosse l'infiammata cortesia / di fra Tommaso e 'l discreto latino; / e mosse meco questa compagna."

[11] Ibid., 7.1.91. "O che Dio solo per sua cortesia / dimesso avesse, o che l'uom per sè isso / avesse sodisfatto a sua follia [Either must God, of His sole courtesy, / Remit, or man must pay with all that's his, / The debt of sin in its entirety]."

DETERMINATION

WINSTON CHURCHILL had the look of a bulldog, and this served him well in successfully transmitting to his people the determination they needed to get through a long and terrible war. He was a great leader but was also a man of unusual versatility: a gifted journalist, a biographer and historian of classic proportions, a talented painter, a pilot, a soldier of courage and distinction, and an orator of rare power. Though he won the Nobel Prize in 1953 for literature, his power of oratory may have been his greatest gift. It seemed that he had been nursing all his gifts so that when the moment came—that "finest hour"—he could lavish them on the salvation of Britain and the values he believed his country stood for in the world. He was an intense patriot who firmly believed in his country's greatness and its historical importance in Europe, the empire, and the world. He possessed an iron constitution, inexhaustible energy, and a capacity for total concentration. What he pledged to his people was direct and unvarnished: "I have nothing to offer but blood, toil, tears and sweat."[1] His words were a vivid expression of his character and virtually infused the virtue of determination in his listeners:

> What is our aim? . . . Victory, victory at all costs, victory in spite of all terror; victory, however long and

[1] *Hansard,* May 13, 1940, col. 1502.

hard the road may be; for without victory, there is no survival.[2]

We shall not flag or fail. We shall go on to the end. We shall fight in France, we shall fight on the seas and oceans, we shall fight with growing confidence and growing strength in the air, we shall defend our island, whatever the cost may be. We shall fight on the beaches, we shall fight on the landing grounds, we shall fight in the fields and in the streets, we shall fight in the hills; we shall never surrender.[3]

Is it possible to account for the development of a man of such extraordinary determination? What was in Churchill's background or upbringing that might shed light on the emergence of England's most powerful personality of the twentieth century?

Winston Churchill was born on November 30, 1874, at Blenheim Palace. His delivery was premature. His father, Lord Randolph, regarded him as useless, and his mother was equally unsympathetic. Such affection as the young Winston received came from his nanny, Mrs. Anne Everest, to whom he was devoted. He suffered from a speech impediment, which he never wholly lost, and was inclined throughout his life to deep depression. His poor academic record at Harrow seemingly justified his father's decision to have him pursue an army career. But it was only on his third attempt that Winston managed to pass the entrance examination to the Royal Military College.

Socially, his parents were publicly ostracized between 1876 and 1884. Theirs was a marriage of convenience, and it was widely known that Lady Randolph was involved in

[2] Ibid.
[3] *Hansard,* June 4, 1940, col. 796.

numerous affairs. Lord Randolph, who had a propensity for gambling, drinking, and overspending, died in 1895 and left only debts.

Some scholars have speculated that it was because of his father's indifference to him that Winston became intensely ambitious and anxious to prove himself.[4] Churchill was actually fond of presenting himself as a deprived and disadvantaged child, further handicapped by a minimal education.

Several analytical and well-respected studies on Churchill's political life conclude that he displayed many faults. It was not uncommon for him to be mistaken in his beliefs, headstrong in his actions, childish in his reactions, and misguided in his decisions. What cannot be disputed, however, is his contribution to British morale and his determination to secure victory for his fellow citizens. As he himself put it, he gave the roar to the British lion. During the years of crisis, his eloquence was of incalculable importance to his countrymen. He not only governed; he inspired.

How does one explain the phenomenon that was Churchill, or any other person, for that matter? One does not. Personality is a mystery. In the dynamic tension between freedom and grace, a unique and completely unpredictable self emerges. The individual person is not the product of his genes, his environment, nor his family tree alone. Churchill himself had an abiding sense of his own spiritual nature and his implacable duty to fulfill his personal destiny. Perhaps his own words bear the clearest testimony to the man who was Sir Winston Leonard Spencer Churchill:

When great causes are on the move in the world, stirring all men's souls, drawing them from their

[4] R. Blake and W. P. Louis, eds., *Churchill* (New York: W. W. Norton, 1993), p. 1.

firesides, casting aside comfort, wealth, and the pursuit of happiness in response to impulses at once awe-striking and irresistible, we learn that we are spirits, not animals, and that something is going on in space and time which, whether we like it or not, spells duty.[5]

Commentary

The kind of determination that is truly virtuous is rare because it presupposes a battery of other virtues. Determination without patience is impetuosity; without hope, it is blindness. If it is not wedded to discernment, it is mere fanaticism; and if it is not united with courage, it is nothing more than stubbornness. Finally, in the absence of fidelity, determination is no more virtuous than compulsive behavior.

To have the virtue of determination, then, a person must be patient, hopeful, discerning, courageous, and faithful to his purpose. Patience gives him the resources to remain committed over a long period of time. Hope allows him to keep sight of his ultimate objective. Discernment lets him know whether he is being wise or foolish. Courage enables him to face danger without cowering. Fidelity binds him to the good he is striving to achieve.

Determination, nourished and protected by its attendant virtues, must not be confused with fanaticism. Churchill noted that the fanatic is a person who cannot change the subject and knows no other. Scholar Richard Weaver spoke of fanaticism as "redoubling one's efforts after one's aim has

[5] Ibid., pp. 514–15.

been forgotten". And the poet William Cowper holds that fanaticism is "the false fire of an overheated brain".

Determination is resolute and proceeds with calmness. It is enlightened and unlikely to burn itself out. It is a remarkably resourceful virtue. Sociologist Steven Goldberg exemplified determination when he suffered sixty-nine rejections by fifty-five different publishers of the manuscript of a book that is now regarded as a classic: *The Inevitability of Patriarchy.* The *Guinness Book of World Records* lists this as a record for the largest number of rejections before the publication of a book that is subsequently critically acclaimed.

Robert Bruce, King of Scotland (1274–1329) also exemplified determination. After being defeated in battle, King Robert was lying on a bed in a hut. He observed a spider trying to swing from one beam on the ceiling to another by one of its threads. The spider failed to execute the maneuver in six consecutive attempts. Robert reflected that he, too, had failed in six successive battles and then vowed that if the spider succeeded in its seventh try, he would fight a seventh battle. The spider executed the swing, and Robert Bruce went forth to victory.

Determination may also be illustrated on a collective level. In Ireland, in the early eighteenth century, a family caught sheltering or housing a schoolteacher was severely punished. Its house would be burned and crops destroyed. The British government at that time was bent on preventing the Irish from becoming educated. In the view of the government, if the Irish were kept ignorant, they would be incapable of rising up to claim their independence.

Not acquiescence to tyranny, however, but a determination to educate was the Irish response. So that people would not lose their property or crops, the Irish "hedge schools" were born. The hedge-school teacher took his students out of doors. He would select some remote corner, the hidden side of a hedge or a mossy bank that protected his pupils from being spotted by passing strangers. A different student was chosen each day to be a lookout and would give the signal if he saw a stranger approaching. When trouble came, teacher and students quickly hid the few books and note-paper they had and scattered until it was safe to reassemble. The itinerant hedge-school teachers are credited with pre-serving the Irish language and much of the poetry and legends of Ireland. Some of these dedicated teachers copied complete books by hand and then loaned them to their students.

From this clandestine and loosely organized background, the brightest or most determined students found their way into the army, the Church, foreign service, and the legal and medical professions by way of European universities. Daniel O'Connell, "The Great Liberator" of Ireland, learned his alphabet in a hedge school in four hours. Matthew Tierney, a nineteenth-century physician who served England's King George IV, is one of the best-known graduates of the hedge schools.

The hedge schools have been described as guerilla war-fare waged against the British government's attempt to keep the Irish uneducated, a battle the determined Irish have convincingly won. Today, Ireland has one of the highest literacy rates in the world—99 percent—a tribute to the lasting legacy of the outlaw hedge schools and good old Irish determination.[6]

---

[6] Maura Ciarrocchi, "To Quench the Thirst for Knowledge", *Our Sunday Visitor,* March 14, 1993.

FAITH

ABORTION IS commonly referred to as a "choice". For
the many who view it in this light, it bears no moral
implication. Choosing to terminate a pregnancy belongs to
the same order as selecting the color of new carpeting or
deciding which wine to serve at dinner. When one makes
such a choice, one does so on the basis of convenience,
personal preference, or the best information that is available,
but not on the basis of faith, especially faith in God! So it
was a revelation for Dianne Klein, a columnist for the *Los
Angeles Times,* to learn about Theresa, who described her
out-of-wedlock pregnancy as a "test of faith".[1]

Theresa (a pseudonym taken from her favorite saint,
Teresa of Avila) was sixteen when she first met her boyfriend,
who would become her first and only lover. Within two
years, despite objections from the boy's family, they were
engaged. They planned to be married within a year. It was
during their engagement that something they had not planned
happened—Theresa became pregnant. Nonetheless, her
untimely pregnancy would not have been particularly problematic had it not been for the fact that in her eighth
week—a critical time in the baby's development—she contracted German measles. Her obstetrician told her about a
child he had delivered a year before whose mother had also

[1] Dianne Klein, "One Woman's Choice: Pregnancy as Test of
Faith", *The Los Angeles Times,* December 3, 1989.

been exposed to German measles. The baby was born deaf and retarded, with his intestines outside his body. He strongly advised Theresa to abort. He warned her that her baby would "be a vegetable, or worse".

Although it was three years before the United States Supreme Court would legalize abortion nationwide, abortion was available at this time in California to women who were believed to be carrying severely deformed fetuses. The doctor's ominous prediction left Theresa dazed. But she decided to place her faith in God and bear the child.

Anticipating the worst for her baby and not wanting to burden her fiancé, Theresa broke off their engagement. A believing Catholic, she spent the last months of her pregnancy at St. Anne's Hospital in Los Angeles, where she "found an inner strength that came from entrusting her situation completely to God".

Moments after she gave birth, the delivering obstetrician asked her in a scolding manner: "Weren't you advised to get an abortion? Well, you should have been." Her son was not breathing, and she barely managed to glimpse his curly dark hair before he was whisked away. His Apgar score, a measure of a newborn's vital signs, was four out of a possible ten (a score greater than seven indicates good health). Although there were no visible signs of a handicap, the child tested positive for measles. Because of the highly contagious nature of the disease, he was placed in isolation.

Theresa decided to have her child adopted, stipulating that he be raised in a Catholic home. She realized that her child, sure to be handicapped, would need a great deal of love. But a few days later, when she was allowed to view her baby from behind a glass wall, her maternal instinct came to the fore. "I *have* to take care of this baby", she vowed.

She and the child's father decided to marry after all. The

newlyweds soon reclaimed their child from his foster mother, an older woman chosen to care for the baby because of her immunity to measles. "Baby has shaking of arms and legs", read the note that the foster mother handed Theresa when she picked up her son. "Do not be alarmed. Just hold him close and talk to him."

On her doctor's advice, Theresa kept her still-contagious son in isolation until he was twelve months old. "As far as I'm concerned", the doctor told her, "you should take that child and lock him in a closet for a year." Until he was five, Theresa kept waiting for something to go wrong, because her obstetrician had told her that even if her baby had seemed normal at birth, "then by age five, something devastating would show up".

The child developed normally, however, and Theresa's faith in God remained firm. Long after the crisis period passed, her son continued to remain normal. In some ways he was supernormal. When his IQ was tested, it was in the 150 range.

At the time Klein informed her readers of the story, Theresa was a thirty-eight-year-old interior designer and her nineteen-year-old son, whom she refers to as one of God's miracles as well as "the most spiritual person she has ever met", had entered the seminary to become a Catholic priest.[2]

[2] This account is reprinted in *The Human Life Review,* Winter 1990, pp. 88–91.

Commentary

Faith is so fundamental that without it we can see nothing. John Dryden's remark that "Reason saw not until faith sprung to life" has been affirmed and reaffirmed by the most eminent of scientists. Norbert Wiener, the "father of cybernetics", enjoins his fellow scientists to have faith that the cosmos is the work of a God who has imprinted it with an intelligible design rather than an undecipherable chaos that can only deceive and confound us. "When we do not know whether a particular phenomenon we observe is the work of God or the work of Satan, the very roots of our faith are shaken. . . . Science is a way of life which can flourish only when men are free to have faith."[3] Einstein speaks of "a superior reasoning power" who is revealed in our "incomprehensible universe". The author of the "Theory of Relativity" frequently reminded his readers that the mystical order, which is an object of faith, takes precedence over the small world that science delineates: "The most beautiful and most profound emotion we can experience is the sensation of the mystical. It is the sower of all true science. He to whom this emotion is a stranger, who can no longer wonder and stand rapt in awe, is as good as dead."[4]

We need faith to have science; more importantly, we need faith in order to have a sense of who we are and where we are going. We need to have faith that there is a place for us in the vast scheme of things. It has been said that without faith we are like stained glass windows in the dark. It accords with our nature to receive light from a higher source that

[3] Norbert Wiener, *The Human Use of Human Beings* (New York: Avon Books, 1967), pp. 262–64.

[4] Quoted in Lincoln Barnett, *The Universe and Dr. Einstein* (New York: William Morrow, 1966), pp. 108–9.

illumines our lives and gives them shape, just as it is in keeping with the design of stained glass windows to transmute the light they receive into meaningful images. Those who lack faith seem to be on the wrong side of things, on the outside looking in, rather than on the inside looking out. They appear to be looking at the heavens through the wrong end of the telescope. Nathaniel Hawthorne has stated the matter most elegantly: "Christian faith is a grand cathedral, with divinely pictured windows—Standing without, you can see no glory, nor can imagine any, but standing within every ray of light reveals a harmony of unspeakable splendors."

"Faith is the substance of things hoped for, the evidence of things that are not seen."[5] It is that which gives a person his fundamental orientation and identity in a world that would otherwise be entirely alien either to plan or person. Faith is our stairway to the stars.

The faith of great men is not so much something they possess as it is something that possesses them. Faith gives us the unshakeable confidence that there is a purpose to our existence, that we should not allow ourselves to be engulfed in the passing waves of disappointment. Faith counteracts fear, overcomes doubt, allays anxiety, complements reason, inspires dedication, releases energy, and offers peace. Without faith, we cannot commence our greatest adventure. In the words of George Santayana:

> Columbus found a world, and had no chart
> Save one that faith deciphered in the skies;
> To trust the soul's invincible surmise
> Was all his science and his only art.

[5] Heb 11:1.

Faith is, for Leo Tolstoy, "the force of Life"; for Walt Whitman, the "antiseptic of the soul"; for Abraham Lincoln, the confidence that "right makes might".

Yet faith is not superstition or credulity. The former is sitting in darkness as opposed to living in the sun, while the latter is assent to what is either preposterous or impossible. "Faith", as Pascal remarks in his *Pensées,* "declares what the senses do not see, but not the contrary of what they see. It is above them, not contrary to them."[6]

Most importantly, we need faith that creation is the product of a loving and provident God. There is faith that we can make sense out of the world of nature, that the cosmos is a home and will not deceive us. There is a higher faith that we are not purposeless tenants in an albeit intelligible universe. Then there is the faith that our personal meaning in an ordered world has its culminating significance in relation to a saving God. We know, live, and find our being in the light of faith. "The steps of faith", as the poet Whitman writes, "fall on the seeming void and find the rock beneath."

Theresa's faith that God had a purpose in creating her son and that she was to help execute that purpose illustrates how faith is indispensable for the emergence of extraordinary things. Had her son been severely deformed, this fact would not have contradicted her faith, nor would it have justified her doctor's recommendation to abort. True faith remains, despite what may appear to be a disappointing outcome. The time-honored rendering of Job 13:15, "Though he will slay me, yet will I trust him", indicates that man should

[6] Blaise Pascal, *Pensées,* trans. Martin Turnell (New York: Harper and Row, 1962), p. 141.

continue to have faith in God even when God "hides his face", so to speak, in witholding signs of his benevolent presence.[7]

People do not always witness the vindication of their faith. But when they do, as in Theresa's case, they have reason to rejoice. We should not judge God when our faith does not seem fruitful to us, but we should express our thanks when it does. This is the stance Gerard Manley Hopkins adopted in response to the dilemma posed by the death of five Franciscan nuns who drowned when their ship foundered. "For I greet him the days I meet him and bless when I understand."[8]

---

[7] *The Jerusalem Bible* (Garden City: Doubleday, 1966), p. 743, n. 13g.

[8] W. H. Gardiner, ed., "The Wreck of the Deutschland", in *Gerard Manley Hopkins: A Selection of His Poems and Prose* (London: Penguin Books, 1953), p. 14.

FIDELITY

THE SON of Lithuanian immigrants, Edward Krauciunas grew up in the Back of the Yards section of Chicago, which was well known for its knockdown-dragout toughness. When he passed through the three ethnic districts that lined the route to his violin lessons, the Irish, Italians, and Poles took turns assaulting him, both on his way there and on his return home. He never succeeded in mastering the violin, but he did become an adept boxer.[1]

His father worked as a butcher and kept Doberman pinschers around to discourage would-be robbers. The family income was never sufficient to create the hope that Edward could ever leave his section of Hogtown to pursue a better life. College was simply unaffordable and, therefore, out of the question.

While playing football for De La Salle Institute, however, he impressed his high-school coach, Norman Barry. It was Barry who, because he had trouble pronouncing Krauciunas, shortened his name to "Krause" and, for good measure, supplied the enduring nickname of "Moose".[2] Barry had played on Notre Dame's undefeated National Championship team in 1920 and was the backfield running-mate of

[1] Moose Krause and Stephen Singular, *Notre Dame's Greatest Coaches* (New York: Simon and Schuster, 1993), pp. 20–21.
[2] Jack Connor, *Leahy's Lads* (South Bend, Ind.: Diamond Communications, 1994).

the legendary George Gipp. He took his protegé to South Bend, Indiana, one weekend and gave him a chance to display his gridiron prowess before the critical eye of his former coach, Knute Rockne.

Rockne liked what he saw and granted Moose Krause an athletic scholarship to Notre Dame.[3] In retrospect, it may have been the soundest investment the university ever made. Moose went on to become an All-American tackle in 1932 and 1933, on both offense and defense. He also was an All-American center in basketball in the three years from 1932 to 1934. He graduated *cum laude* with a degree in journalism. After graduation, he coached the university's basketball team for eight seasons. He distinguished himself as "Mr. Notre Dame" during his long tenure—from 1949 to 1981—as the school's athletic director. Though he is one of many Notre Dame alumni to have been inducted into the Football Hall of Fame, he is its only alumnus to have been enshrined in the Basketball Hall of Fame.

In 1967, shortly after returning from Rome, where Edward Krause, Jr., was ordained a priest in the Holy Cross Order, tragedy struck. Moose's wife, Elise, was seriously injured when a young man, driving under the influence of alcohol, ran a stop sign and rammed the rear of her taxi. She suffered severe damage to two regions of the brain, one affecting memory and the other, emotional control. Doctors did not expect her to survive the night. Moose, however, repeatedly expressed his certainty that his wife would not die.

She indeed survived, living for an additional twenty-

---

[3] Edward W. "Moose" Krause, "The Game That Mimics Life", *Notre Dame Magazine,* vol. 15, no. 3 (Autumn 1987).

three years. She was in intensive care for four months, came home for a long period of convalescence, and spent her last eight years in a nursing home. During this final period, Moose visited her at least twice a day, spoon-feeding her when she could not feed herself and singing to her when she was no longer able to speak. They celebrated their fiftieth wedding anniversary in the nursing home. Moose donned a white tuxedo, and he and his wife renewed their marriage vows.

It was Moose's uncomplaining fidelity and devotion to his wife that prompted Notre Dame President Rev. Theodore Hesburgh, C.S.C., to say to Edward, Jr.: "Your father has had many public successes in life, but nothing is more important in God's eyes than how he cared for your mother for all those years."[4]

Moose Krause was a giant and a legend who had distinguished himself in a sport where giants were commonplace and at a school where legends were customary. Yet these marks of distinction, extraordinary as they are, take a distant second place when compared with the fidelity he showed to his wife, Elise. The world was familiar with his media image, but those close to him saw something far more impressive. In the words of another Notre Dame immortal, former head football coach Ara Parseghian:

His dedication to his faith and to his marriage vows are to be admired and emulated. No one could have been more devoted to his wife than Ed was in the long years after an unfortunate automobile accident robbed her of a normal life. In those years, Moose was able to serve his wife and able to fulfill all her needs.

[4] Krause and Singular, *Notre Dame's Greatest Coaches,* pp. 150–51.

There was no better demonstration of great devotion to family and his religion.[5]

Moose never lacked for opportunities or inducements to enjoy a broader social life than what his wife's nursing home could offer. When he kept turning down requests to travel with the team or to go off on golf holidays, he wondered if people sometimes felt sorry for him. To his son, Edward, Jr., he once said: "It's my responsibility to take care of your mother—there's nowhere I'd rather be than in the room with your mother."[6]

Fidelity is a more immediate expression of love than the desire for happiness.[7] This is something that was known to our primal parents. Eve's sin occurred prior to Adam's. During that interim between sins, Adam may very well have felt that it was better to accompany his wife east of Eden than to remain in Paradise without her. The desire to be with the one whom one loves is more urgent and demanding than the desire for one's own happiness. Far from feeling sorry for Moose, those who knew him well both admired and envied him.

[5] Ibid., p. 246.

[6] Personal communication from Rev. Edward Krause, Jr., C.S.C., October 31, 1994, Gannon University, Erie, Penn.

[7] Krause, "Game": "The heaviest adversity in my life was when my wife was paralyzed in an automobile accident. For four months she lay close to death. Now, after her partial recovery and years of confinement in a nursing home, we carry on together, but it has been a veritable crucifixion for both of us."

Commentary

Fidelity is the virtue that allows us to persevere in living out an unswerving commitment. This pledge of fidelity may take place on any of three distinct levels. We can speak of a commitment to a task, to an ideal such as justice, truth, or beauty, and to another person, as epitomized by Moose Krause in the way he lived out his marriage to his wife, Elise.

Contemporary society offers three major objections to practicing this virtue. First, it regards fidelity as incompatible with freedom; secondly, it argues that no one has either the right or the duty to bind himself to an unknown future; finally, it holds that fidelity might prove unfruitful and therefore could represent a significant waste of time.

These objections are evident in current attitudes that question the value of fidelity in marriage. People want to retain the freedom to divorce in principle and especially in circumstances where undesirable changes arise or more attractive alternatives appear. They want the freedom to divorce in the event they cease wanting to be married to each other or develop a preference for the single state or marriage to a different person.

None of these objections, however, is really aimed at the heart of fidelity. Fidelity maintains its covenant of commitment independently of peripheral eventualities. Nonetheless, most if not all great accomplishments, in the arts, sciences, and human relationships, would not have come about without fidelity. Indeed, great accomplishments presuppose fidelity. But in the absence of any assurance that fidelity will lead to such a positive benefit, people recoil, lose heart, and begin to express their misgivings about losing freedom, binding themselves to the unknown, and wasting time. Such fears and negative preoccupations, however, are wholly unproductive. They immobilize and remove all hope.

Fidelity is not contrary to freedom. In fact, there could be no fidelity without freedom. Unless a pledge, promise, or commitment is made from a basis of freedom, it is entirely meaningless. The policy of asking public servants to take oaths implicitly honors their capacity to commit themselves freely to the common good. The marriage vow, expressed by the words "I do", represents a gift of self that is freely given. Moreover, it implies a continuing renewal over the course of a lifetime. The vow that is made in freedom must also be ever renewed in that same spirit. To make a vow and live up to it demands a particularly high degree of freedom. It also implies that one knows that freedom itself is not a terminal value but has meaning only insofar as it is directed toward a higher good.

Although the future is unknown, it is unrealistic never to act in any committed fashion unless we first secure some guarantee that it will necessarily bring about desirable results. As the Danish philosopher Søren Kierkegaard has rightly pointed out, we live forward while we learn backward. The future is not merely a reenactment of the past. It is a horizon of novelty and surprise alongside of defeat and disappointment.

Before we make a serious commitment, it should be emphasized, we must first have a great deal of knowledge about who we are and what we can do. Fidelity demands as much self-knowledge as it does freedom. It also demands courage and hope.

A vow may, indeed, prove unproductive. A spouse may die before the honeymoon is over. A commitment to a particular vocation or course of studies or career may, because of unforeseeable circumstances, be unsustainable. Nonetheless, we must understand that the essential beauty of fidelity lies not so much in its capacity to promise favorable results as in its courage, its hopefulness, and its extraordinary faith in the providential order of things and in the potentialities of each human being. Mother Teresa's words offer comfort as well as insight in this regard: "God does not ask us to be successful but to be faithful."

The absence of any capacity to express fidelity results in dissipation rather than freedom, inconstancy rather than realism, and inertia rather than practicality.

The great Christian existentialist Gabriel Marcel assigns a particularly high place to fidelity. We can be faithful to our vows, according to Marcel, not because we have any surety concerning the future states of our feelings, but because we can transcend the moments of our life-flux and express our loyalty to God and, in God, to our fellowmen. It is in God's presence that a pledge bearing on the future is made.

The soul is in search of its own integrity, or, in religious language, its salvation. The soul cannot find such authenticity by acting for nothing other than what is guaranteed. The complete avoidance of fidelity must inevitably bring about despair. The soul must act in faith, and it must act in accordance with an invocation of the transcendent.[8] Out of essential humility, man recognizes that he is a creaturely being and not an autonomous god. His fidelity, by which he unites himself with the transcendent, is truly a "creative fidelity", one that allows him to realize, more and more, his being and his destiny.

[8] Gabriel Marcel, *Creative Fidelity,* trans. Robert Rosthal (New York: Farrar, Straus, 1964) The original title of this work is *Du refus à l'invocation,* p. 167.

Those who criticize fidelity do so from want of other virtues, such as self-knowledge, humility, courage, hope, loyalty to God and neighbor, faith in the ultimate scheme of things. If we dare reject fidelity itself, however it is expressed— toward a task, an ideal, or another person—we cannot help but fall into an abyss of despair.

GENEROSITY

JEAN VALJEAN, the hero of Victor Hugo's *Les Misérables,* had spent nineteen years in the galleys: five years for stealing a loaf of bread to feed the starving children of his widowed sister, and fourteen for attempting to escape on four separate occasions. The yellow passport he received upon his release and which he was obliged to present to potential employers made it almost certain that no one would ever hire him, for it read, "This man is very dangerous." A return to crime and reincarceration seemed inevitable.

On the fourth day after his release, he had journeyed a great distance on foot without having had anything to eat. When evening came, his hunger and fatigue were made even more intolerable by a cold rain that chilled his body. But he was rejected, rudely and repeatedly, wherever he sought food or lodging. Finally, a sympathetic stranger advised him to knock on the door of the bishop's house. When he did, Bishop Bienvenu welcomed him with a show of kindness that was unknown to the ex-prisoner. Valjean's countenance lit up when the bishop referred to him as *"Monsieur",* for this form of address to a convict was like a glass of water to a man dying of thirst. Ignominy craves respect. "This is not my house," Bienvenu explained to him, "it is the house of Christ. It does not ask any comer whether he has a name, but whether he has an affliction.

You are suffering; you are hungry and thirsty; be welcome . . . whatever is here is yours." In this respect, as the bishop further elucidated, he knew Valjean's name even before he met him: "Your name is my brother."[1]

The bishop treated his guest royally. He entertained him and fed him; and when the meal was over, he ushered him to his quarters. Valjean slept soundly but only for about four hours. What awakened him was too good a bed. For he had not slept in a bed for nearly twenty years. He awoke in a perturbed state of mind. Memories swirled pell-mell, crossing each other confusedly, losing their shapes and then disappearing as if in a muddy and troubled stream. One thought finally emerged to drive all other thoughts away. It was the six silver plates that had graced the supper table and were now in the bishop's sleeping chamber only a few feet away. They had taken possession of him. As solid, old silver, they would bring a handsome price, more than he had received for his nineteen years' labor. His mind wavered for a long time before he finally came to his decision. With the stealthy carefulness of a cat, he slipped into the bishop's room, removed the plates from the cupboard, and fled the house.

The next morning three gendarmes appeared at Bienvenu's door holding Valjean by the collar. They had arrested him, inspected his knapsack, and found the plates, which their fugitive said the bishop had given to him. Bienvenu acted swiftly; he knew exactly what was at stake. He spoke directly to his overnight guest without greeting the police: "Ah, there you are! I am glad to see you. But! I gave you the candlesticks also, which are silver like the rest, and would

---

[1] Victor Hugo, *Les Misérables,* trans. Charles E. Wilbour (New York: Modern Library, 1990), pp. 65–66.

bring you two hundred francs. Why did you not take them along with your plates?"[2]

Valjean was dumbfounded. The gendarmes, respecting the bishop's word, released their suspect and went away. Bienvenu then withdrew the candlesticks from the mantel and presented them to Valjean, who was trembling in every limb. "Forget not, never forget that you have promised me to use this silver to become an honest man", Bienvenu said. "Jean Valjean, my brother," he continued solemnly, "you belong no longer to evil, but to good. It is your soul that I am buying for you. I withdraw it from dark thoughts and from the spirit of perdition, and I give it to God."[3]

It was the turning point in the life of Valjean, though it took some time before he could grasp the full spiritual significance of the bishop's generosity. Nearing the end of his life, he bequeathed the two candlesticks to his adopted daughter, Cosette. Though they were, in fact, silver, to him they were gold, even diamond. They had come to symbolize not only the bishop's generosity but his own redemption. "They change the candles which are put into them", he said, "into consecrated tapers." At this moment his thoughts returned to Bienvenu. "I do not know whether he who gave them to me is satisfied with me in heaven. I have done what I could."[4] In his last words to Cosette and her husband, Marius, and in a manner worthy of the good bishop, he said: "Love each other dearly always. There is scarcely anything else in the world but that: to love one another."[5]

[2] Ibid., p. 89.
[3] Ibid., p. 90.
[4] Ibid., p. 1220.
[5] Ibid., p. 1221.

Commentary

True generosity demands a measure of self-sacrifice. To give away something that one has no use for or would readily throw away does not capture the essence of generosity. When the good bishop gave away the silver plates, his housekeeper complained that their remaining serviceware left much to be desired—the tin plates had a disagreeable smell, while the iron plates had an unpleasant taste. "Well," said Bienvenu, "then, wooden plates."[6]

At the same time, generosity does not impoverish the giver. Rather, it enriches him a hundredfold. His good deeds bear fruit in his own heart as well as in the hearts of those to whom he has been generous.

The great enemy of generosity is greed, which is an excessive desire for personal security. But it is an illusion to think that greed is consistent with security. In the motion picture *Wall Street*, millionaire financier Gordon Gecko pays homage to greed before a docile throng of like-minded businessmen. "Greed is good", he tells them. It is "natural, clean, and healthy". It is what makes the economy strong. Gecko's anxiety intensifies as his fortune increases until he finally breaks down. His greed, rather than leading him to security, brings about his personal and moral disintegration as well as the loss of his financial empire.

Leo Tolstoy writes about this same paradoxical relationship between greed and ruin in his short story "Much Land". In this tale, the devil overhears the peasant Pakhom make an idle boast: "Only give me land, and I fear no man—no, not even the Devil himself."[7] The devil appears to Pakhom in a series of disguises, each time offering

[6] Ibid., p. 89.
[7] Leo Tolstoy, "Much Land", in *The Works of Tolstoy* (New York: Walter Black, 1928).

him more land at cheaper prices. In his final appearance, he offers the peasant as much land as he can circle on foot between dawn and sundown for a mere one thousand roubles. The peasant, however, would forfeit all the land if he failed to return to his starting point by sunset.

Pakhom is intoxicated with the prospect of owning so large an area of rich land. Knowing he must be back before the sun sets, his plan is prudent and practical. But his greed does not allow him to resist taking more and more land. After awhile, he begins to fear that he will not be able to return to his starting point in time to claim everything: "Surely I have not taken in too much land even to get back, however much I hurry?"

The Bashkirs are waiting for him. He returns, utterly exhausted, and collapses at their feet, dead of a heart attack. The devil, in the guise of the Starshina, is laughing. "Bury him", he commands, and his fellow Bashkirs obey as they roll the body into an open grave that is the same length as Pakhom from head to heels. How much land does a man need? The mordant answer is: no more than what is needed to bury him.

Through generosity, one expands his soul. Through greed, one contracts it. Pascal understood that man's true nature is expressed, not by any material acquisition, such as land, but by dint of his spirituality. In his *Pensées* he writes: "It is not from space that I must seek my dignity, but from the control of my thought. I should not have more of it through the possession of land. By means of space the universe contains me and swallows me up like a speck: by means of thought I comprehend the universe."[8]

Material possessions do not add to the humanity of a person. They belong to the sphere of "I-It" relationships, to

[8] Blaise Pascal, *Pensées,* trans. Martin Turnell (New York: Harper and Row, 1962), p. 94.

use the terminology of Martin Buber. Man needs to have things in order to live, but he needs to cultivate the spiritual plane of "I-Thou" relationships in order to be human. Without "It", man cannot live, but "It" alone cannot make man human.[9]

The distinguished physician and psychiatrist Paul Tournier of Switzerland writes about a man who, like Jean Valjean, found renewed hope in life through a single act of generosity. This man, hungry and destitute, was in flight from the Nazis who had invaded his country. In the street he saw an itinerant vendor selling buns, but he had no money with which to buy any. A wretched beggar came up and bought one himself and then, turning and seeing him there, offered it to him instead of eating it himself. It revealed to him the true life of the spiritualized person he had been looking for. It was a decisive moment in his life and made a better man of him.[10]

At the heart of man's being is a law of superabundance, writes the personalist philosopher Jacques Maritain. The generosity that springs from this center, which goes far beyond what ordinary justice would require, resembles the generosity of God.[11] God creates, not from obligation, but from generosity. It is in practicing the virtue of generosity that man most closely resembles the creative God in whose image he has been made.

[9] Martin Buber, *I–Thou,* trans. Ronald Smith (New York: Charles Scribner's, 1958), p. 34.

[10] Paul Tournier, *The Meaning of Persons,* trans. Edwin Hudson (New York: Harper and Row, 1957), p. 31.

[11] Jacques Maritain, *An Introduction to the Basic Problems of Moral Philosophy,* trans. Cornelia N. Borgenhoff (Albany, N.Y.: Magi Books, 1990), pp. 168–9.

GRACIOUSNESS

THERE ARE JUST a handful more than a hundred neuro-surgeons practicing in Canada. Dr. Harley Smyth is one of the best and most highly respected of this relatively small fraternity. But when it comes to dealing with the pituitary gland, that mysterious organ the size and shape of a lima bean, situated at the base of the brain, he is arguably *the* best.[1] Smyth, however, finds such comparisons invidious. His interest is not in status. The principle by which he practices his highly intricate art is the one that Albert Schweitzer adopted: *Ehrfurcht vor dem Leben* (reverence for life).

Smyth understands only too well how easy it is for authority to become superiority, and he strives to resist this temptation. "There is a certain disdain", he says, "by some doctors for the laity. I have no doubt that medicine sometimes attracts people who are unconsciously looking for a place from which they can exercise power over people."[2]

Some doctors are better at rounds than others, but Smyth is superb. He is so tuned-in to his many Italian patients, for example, that he has picked up enough Italian during his bedside chats to carry on cheerful, if clumsy, conversations. He has an extraordinary memory for not only the names of his patients but also the names of their relatives. His abiding

[1] Martin O'Malley, *Doctors* (Toronto: Macmillan, 1983), p. 28.
[2] Ibid., p. 26.

awareness that, more often than not, he is holding his patients' lives in his hands leads him to pray before every surgical intervention. Taped to the inside of his locker door are the words Sir Jacob Astly wrote before the battle of Newberry:

> Lord,
> I shall be verie busie this day:
> I may forget Thee
> But doe not Thou forget me.

Smyth's commitment to the "reverence for life" principle includes his defense of the unborn. His practice as a neurosurgeon fully corroborates his view that the unborn child warrants respect. He cites, for example, an occasion when he operated on a twenty-three-year-old woman who was bleeding from a malformed thin-walled artery in her brain during the fifth month of her first pregnancy. The procedure took eleven hours. The twelve-member team included two anesthetists and two obstetricians who kept unbroken vigil over each movement and heartbeat of the unborn child. Four months after the operation, the baby was delivered normally; both the child and the mother were fine. "Life is a gift", according to Smyth, "of which we may become, over a short season, loving caretakers and loyal stewards."[3]

Around the same time that Smyth began his witness for life, his wife was pregnant with their third child. She knew intuitively that something was wrong, and when her little girl, Anna, was born, they discovered she had Down's syndrome. "It was ironic", said Dr. Smyth, "that I, who had been an advocate for the unborn, had been called to

[3] Harley Smyth, *The Human Life Review,* Winter 1976, p. 99.

the witness stand. The timing was breathtaking."[4] When some of his colleagues suggested that he institutionalize his daughter at age three, when she would be entitled to free care, the very idea repulsed him and prompted him to ask: "In the elimination of the obvious heartache involved in the receiving of a mentally retarded child into the family of man, what *else* might we eliminate?"[5] In due time this question was answered for him in a most dramatic and personal way, for the "something else" that might have been eliminated was his very own life.

Smyth was devoted to his daughter. In fact, he sometimes introduced himself at public appearances as "Anna's dad". Despite his eighty-hour work week, he always managed to spend time with her. In particular, he was fond of taking her to an indoor pool for swimming lessons. One day at the pool, his then seven-year-old daughter noticed a "freckle" on his back that looked different from the others. She noticed it again the next time they went swimming, and said, "Doctor fix it!" Because of Anna's insistence, Smyth asked a plastic surgeon at the hospital where he worked to examine the curious spot. The "freckle" proved to be a malignant melanoma, a dangerous form of skin cancer. Because it was treated at an early stage, the doctors gave Dr. Smyth a good prognosis.[6]

Today, a dozen years later, Smyth is still practicing neurosurgery, and with no appreciable reduction in his work hours. Moreover, he has not lost his gracious willingness to be led, especially by his daughter. Now nineteen years of age, Anna continues to lead her father, as he puts it,

[4] O'Malley, p. 18.
[5] Martin O'Malley, "A Doctor's Dilemma", *Saturday Night,* May 1983, p. 23.
[6] Ibid., p. 29.

"onto unusual paths and into unusual places". Recently, in March of 1995, he accompanied her to a special school in Camphill Village, Ontario. There, with fifty others—half of whom were handicapped, and most of these nonverbal— they spent two weeks together in community giving witness to what Smyth describes as "magic moments of complete teamwork". Smyth's own role, which he accepted with both graciousness and pride, was to keep the fire going for the maple syrup.[7]

Commentary

Being gracious can prove to be a lifesaver in more ways than one. The distinguished psychiatrist Viktor Frankl was awakened once at 3:00 A.M. by a telephone call from a complete stranger. The caller was a distraught woman who spoke incoherently for about twenty minutes about committing suicide. Frankl, though extremely groggy, listened to the woman until she concluded the conversation. Some time later, the woman met Frankl and thanked him profusely for saving her life. Frankl recalled the telephone incident but pleaded that he had been too sleepy at the time to have told her anything that could possibly have been helpful. The woman heartily agreed, remarking that she could not make head or tail of what he was trying to say. "But", she added, "the very fact that a great man such as you would spend twenty minutes on the phone at three o'clock in the morning with a complete stranger such as myself meant that I must be important in some way, and so I decided to go on living."

[7] Personal communication with Dr. Smyth, April 3, 1995.

Graciousness is the largeness of heart that allows a person, no matter how outstanding he is in a particular field, to remain in touch with the essential humanity of others. It keeps him from taking himself and his achievements so seriously that he forgets everyone else.

Toward the end of his life, Artur Rubinstein heard much about the prowess of twelve-year-old piano prodigy Dmitris Sgouros. Though he had always been suspicious of child prodigies, he graciously invited the boy to play for him at his home in Geneva. Happy and honored to oblige, Sgouros gave a two-hour concert for his audience of one. As the final note died away, Rubinstein, considered the last of the great romantic pianists, declared the lad a better pianist than himself.[8]

The antithesis of snobbery, graciousness flows from a disposition of benevolence and, in its clearest manifestations, bestows honor and respect on those who have no personal, social, or professional claim to such largess. The person who displays snobbery prefers what separates people from each other rather than what unites them. He ranks his fellowmen according to how important they appear to be in terms of their wealth, occupation, social standing, and the like. He does not "waste his time" on those beneath him but seeks recognition from those above. He deems not being obliged to return telephone calls a clear sign of success.

The gracious person, on the other hand, is a democrat in the truest sense of the term. He does not allow class or other distinctions to prevent him from seeing the worth in others. He does not allow his personal, professional, or social advantages to alienate him from his "inferiors". Gra-

---

[8] *Reader's Digest,* January 1986.

ciousness presupposes the ability to see grace in everyone and respond appropriately.

U.S. President John F. Kennedy expressed graciousness when he introduced himself to the French as the husband who had accompanied his wife, Jackie, to Paris. Louise Fletcher exhibited the same virtue when, after receiving an Academy Award for her role in *One Flew over the Cuckoo's Nest,* she used sign language to thank her deaf parents for giving her a dream that they now could see had been realized. And General Charles de Gaulle was so gracious a man that, even when preoccupied with political matters of historic and global significance, he managed to make time for his daughter with Down's syndrome, delighting her with his singing and dancing.[9]

Pride often interferes with our capacity to see the evidence of grace in others. When our vision becomes limited to our own exertions and accomplishments, we have difficulty acknowledging that God is the source of all that is good. We then also fail to see the gifts he bestows generously, albeit differently, to everyone else.

During the American Civil War, President Abraham Lincoln proclaimed a national day of "Humiliation, Fasting, and Prayer". On that day in 1863, Lincoln stated that although Americans had been the recipients of the choicest bounties of heaven, they had forgotten God, the source of all those blessings. "We have forgotten the gracious hand which preserved us in peace and multiplied and enriched and strengthened us, and we have vainly imagined, in the deceitfulness of our hearts, that all these blessings were produced

[9] Robert and Suzanne Massie, *Journey* (New York: Knopf, 1973), p. 355.

by some superior wisdom and virtue of our own. Intoxicated with unbroken success, we have become too self-sufficient to feel the necessity of redeeming and preserving grace, too proud to pray to the God that made us."[10]

The drowsy father who walks the baby in the wee hours of the morning, knowing he has a full day of important business ahead, and the young mother who subordinates her professional pursuits to the needs of her newborn mirror to their children the graciousness of God. Graciousness is essential to motherhood and fatherhood, but it is not essential to a career. A careerist who is a snob may improve his standing in the world, but he will be marred by an inherent misanthropy. His will be merely the appearance of success, under which will lie a failure in humanity.

In the movie *The Miracle of Our Lady of Fatima,* the villagers dismiss the three children who claim to have seen the Blessed Mother with such remarks as, "I'm sure the Mother of God has more important things to do than speak to children." They overlook a truth we easily lose sight of ourselves—there is nothing that should be more important to a mother than speaking with her children. In a debate over the merits of feminism, Gloria Steinem asked, "Who wants to be locked up all day with the intellect of a three-year-old?" Her opponent, Midge Decter, like a true mother retorted, "Three-year-olds are some of the most enchanting people in the world", and she added that she would not mind being locked up with one of them any day. We should not forget that Christianity came into the world because a woman was willing to make a child the center of her life.

---

[10] Roy Basler, ed., *The Collected Works of Abraham Lincoln,* vol. 6 (New Brunswick, N.J.: Rutgers University Press, 1953), pp. 155–56.

Through graciousness, which begins with the recognition that there is something other than ourselves that is graced, we come to realize the deeper source of grace that lies within us.

GRATITUDE

"KURELEK'S LIFE is one of the strangest stories ever told."[1] So begins Patricia Morley's official biography of William Kurelek, who, at the time of his death in 1977, was easily Canada's most popular and prolific painter. "Kurelek is", as Dr. Morley acknowledges, "one of the great painters which this country has nurtured."[2]

Kurelek's talent for portraying the essence of common human experiences led journalists to dub him "The People's Painter". He painted farm scenes, many of them set in Western Canada where he grew up. His depictions of people at work and at play are in the tradition of the Renaissance Flemish masters. He was a "message painter" and possessed a remarkable ability to turn his paintings into stories. Like Pieter Brueghel and Hieronymus Bosch, the two painters he most admired, his vision was both social and religious, even mystical.

But there was a dark side to Kurelek's personality. Much of his difficulty stemmed from rejection by his father, a stern man of the soil, who belittled and humiliated his son for not living up to his expectations. Dmytro Kurelek had little patience for and less understanding of his son's artistic

[1] Patricia Morley, *Kurelek: A Biography* (Toronto: Macmillan, 1986), p. 1.
[2] Patricia Morley, "William Kurelek: The Man and the Myth", *Canadian Ethnic Studies,* 16, 3, 84, p. 27.

temperament. As far as he was concerned, William was simply an impractical dunderhead. Kurelek became broodingly introspective, a trait that remained with him all his life.

In an attempt to exorcise his demons of self-doubt and rejection, Kurelek turned to writing his autobiography, a project that began when he was twenty and continued, through two publications and continual revisions, until his death thirty years later. But his paintings were his chief means of communicating with others. They were also a means of communicating with God. In the assessment of his biographer, "they reflected his gratitude and awe in ways that were beyond words."[3]

Kurelek's story is an odyssey that moves from self-doubt to despair and then from recovery to gratitude. It has strong affinities with Francis Thompson's "The Hound of Heaven", a poem that had long been a favorite with Kurelek. According to Kurelek, no other poem expressed so completely his "personal life lesson". He attached particular significance to the line "Nature, poor stepdame, cannot slake my drouth." Like Thompson, Kurelek tells a story whose main episodes are fear and flight, grace and gratitude.

In 1950, Kurelek was hitchhiking to Mexico in search of a master painter. Caught in the cold night air of the Arizona desert, he took refuge under a road bridge and fell asleep. He records in his autobiography that the next thing he realized was that someone was with him, a man in a long, white robe who was urging him to rise: "Get up, we must look after the sheep, or you will freeze to death."[4]

[3] Morley, *Kurelek*, p. 8.
[4] William Kurelek, *Someone with Me* (Ithaca, N.Y.: Cornell Univ. Press, 1973), p. 254.

Kurelek took this vision as a convincing sign that he was not alone, that Someone would always be with him, Someone who had asked him "to get up because there is work to be done".[5]

His experience in the Arizona desert notwithstanding, Kurelek's fortunes then took a turn for the worse. He entered a psychiatric hospital in England to rid himself of chronic depression and acute eye pains. He underwent a series of excruciating electric convulsion treatments. His condition deteriorated. At one point, in the depths of moral despair, he attempted suicide. His life was saved when a hospital orderly entered his room at a propitious moment.

The events that followed led Kurelek to a path he would never forsake. He was introduced to the Catholic faith by a sympathetic occupational therapist. After a period of intense and critical study, he entered the Catholic Church. Filled with a sense of gratitude to God for rescuing him from despair and granting him a life of love, purpose, and success, he decided to use his talents to spread Christ's saving message to the four corners of the globe.

He then spent six years planning and executing 160 paintings to illustrate as many verses in the "Passion of Christ" according to Saint Matthew. His research included a three-week sojourn in the Holy Land, where he retraced the footsteps of Christ, and three years studying the Gospel. He commenced work on New Year's Day in 1960, painting one panel a week until the project was completed. Slides were made from the series and shown by missionaries in various parts of the world. The original paintings now

[5] Ibid., p. 523.

form the centerpiece of the Niagara Falls Art Gallery and Museum, where they are on permanent display.[6]

Kurelek continued to express his gratitude throughout the rest of his life. He donated to the poor a great deal of the money he earned from the sale of his paintings. He adopted foster children, supported farms in Third World countries, and continued to express, by brush and pen, the Good News of Christ's redemption.

Commentary

Gratitude is closely linked with graciousness. Both have a common etymological root in the Greek word for "grace", which is *charis,* meaning "the release of loveliness". Graciousness responds to grace with due respect. Gratitude responds with thanks. Graciousness is reverence, while gratitude is recompense. It is said that gratitude is the memory of the heart. But it is also the homage of the heart that expresses itself in an act of thanksgiving.

There is a line of development that begins with *recognition* and proceeds to *appreciation* and then culminates in *gratitude.* The first is the mere acknowledgment that something is good, the second is the positive impact that good has on the moral sensibilities, the third is a rational and emotional expression of thanks. Moreover, gratitude must always be expressed to another person. We cannot be truly happy or at home in the universe if we consider ourselves cosmic orphans with no one to thank for the gift of life.

Cicero held that gratitude is the mother of all virtues

[6] William Kurelek, *Passion of Christ* (Niagara Falls, Ont.: Niagara Falls Art Gallery and Museum, 1975), foreword, p. 8.

and man's capital duty. This notion of the primacy of gratitude has special application in characterizing our relationship with God. According to an ancient Jewish legend, when God finished creation, he asked the angels what they thought of it. One of them replied that the world is so vast and so perfect that there was nothing wanting, except a voice to offer God that which is owed him, an expression of gratitude.

In heaven, according to Christian theology, the principal prayer of the blessed is thanksgiving. Padre Martinez, a Peruvian Jesuit, believed that gratitude is so highly fitting as a response to God's munificence that he trained himself to say *Deo gratias* (thanks be to God) four hundred times a day, and he encouraged others to do the same.[7]

Gratitude is the first thing a person should do in response to the last thing that God works. Just as an audience applauds a good performance with immediacy and enthusiasm, so too should man praise God's creation. Nonetheless, though thanksgiving can be appropriate, it is certainly not automatic. Even when a person is the recipient of a great gift, he may be unaccountably delinquent in expressing appreciation. It is an old story.

Luke (17:12–19) recounts the story of the ten lepers whom Jesus cured. What remains most striking about this episode is not the miraculous cure but why only one of the ten returned to offer thanks. Christ asks: "Were not all ten made clean? The other nine, where are they?" We sense disappointment in these words. We are puzzled. It would seem that a person who is suddenly and completely cured of such a dreadful affliction as leprosy would be only too eager to give thanks. We even suspect that it would bring

---

[7] Raoul Plus, S.J., *Some Rare Virtues,* trans. Sister Mary Meyer, O.S.F. (Westminster, Minn.: Newman Press, 1950), p. 11.

him joy to give thanks. Yet only one of the ten did, a foreigner from Samaria.

Gratitude appears to be the easiest of all virtues. What does it cost to say "thank you" in return for a favor? It is as good a bargain as we will ever get. Therefore, the vice of ingratitude is something of an enigma. The metaphysical poet George Herbert refers to this troubling human reluctance to express thanks when he writes, "Thou hast given so much to me. Give me one more thing—a grateful heart."

Parents instruct their children to say "thank you" for every favor they receive. Omitting this courtesy is a transgression parents simply cannot tolerate. "What do you say, Jimmy, for the nice sweater Grandma made for you?" Parents do not relent until they succeed in squeezing out of their child a verbal, if not heartfelt, expression of thanks. And it is right that parents behave this way. Children should be taught to be grateful from the earliest age. Gratitude is the first step a child takes in establishing a moral relationship with his elders, just as generosity initiates their moral relationship with him.

Since gratitude is the first virtue parents try to inculcate in their children, the presence of ingratitude suggests the absence of a proper filial spirit. And this disposition of inappreciativeness can prove to be quite painful to disappointed parents. "How sharper than a serpent's tooth it is", writes Shakespeare, "to have a thankless child."[8] We are left to wonder whether the thankless lepers occasioned a similar pain in their Master. We may also wonder whether gratitude is a greater perfection than health. Health is a physical or psychological perfection, whereas gratitude represents perfection on a moral level.

[8] William Shakespeare, *King Lear*, 1.4.310–11.

It is a matter of justice to return what one owes. But it is also a matter of justice, though a higher form of justice, to be grateful for another's generosity. We can be legally compelled to render justice in the strict sense. But we cannot be compelled to fulfill the higher law of justice that generosity requires. Gratitude can flow from a source only in freedom.

By definition, we do not deserve what is given to us out of generosity. We have no claim to be treated generously, whereas we do have a right to be treated in accordance with *quid pro quo* justice. Although we should be satisfied with justice, we should be elated by generosity. And if we are humble enough, we will want to indicate our gratitude rather than feign an illusory self-sufficiency.

Gratitude is surely not as common as it ought to be. People are more likely to complain about what they do not have than be grateful for their blessings. They are more apt to grumble about the thorns on roses than give thanks for the roses among thorns. They are especially unappreciative when things come to them without fanfare and in an accustomed manner. They simply take most things—from sunlight to sunflowers—for granted.

Henrik Ibsen's play *When We Dead Awaken* centers on two characters who hardly notice they are alive. Rubek is a sculptor who, in struggling to create his masterpiece, is oblivious to the world around him. Irene, his model and mistress, fails to capture his love because he is more interested in the Ideal Woman than in one who is mortal. Her fatal flaw is her willingness to be subordinated to an idea. At the end of the play, Irene begins to say something to Rubek but suddenly breaks off: "We only recognize the things we've lost, when—" Rubek looks at her inquiringly and bids her to finish her statement. "When we dead awaken."

He shakes his head sadly, then asks: "And, then—what do we see?" "We see", says Irene, "that we have never lived."[9]

Rubek and Irene failed to value either their life or its inherent potentialities. Their absence of gratitude for what they had and what they could have had led them to seek an impossible ideal that could never be theirs. We must appreciate life before we can be grateful for it. And we must be grateful for life before we can live it authentically.

[9] Henrik Ibsen, *When We Dead Awaken,* in *The Wild Duck and Other Plays,* trans. Eva Le Galliene (New York: Modern Library, 1961), p. 489.

HOLINESS

THERE WAS ONCE a rabbi who had a reputation, which had spread throughout the Jewish village in Russia where he lived, of being unusually holy. Because of his great name, the humble and devoted villagers offered a quaint explanation for why their beloved rabbi disappeared for several hours every Friday morning. In their simple faith, they came to the conclusion that during these hours, their rabbi ascended to heaven and talked with God.

When a newcomer arrived in town and heard this story, he was skeptical. Determined to find out the truth concerning the rabbi's whereabouts on Friday mornings and to explode the villagers' sacred myth, he decided to stalk this man of reputed holiness in order to ascertain the facts for himself. And so, one Friday morning, he hid near the rabbi's house, watched him rise, say his prayers, and put on the clothes of a peasant. He then observed him take an axe with him into the forest where he proceeded to chop down a tree and gather together a large bundle of wood. The newcomer followed the rabbi to a shack located in the very poorest section of the village. There, in this dilapidated dwelling lived an old woman and her son, who was quite ill. The rabbi left them the wood, which was enough to last for a week. After completing his labor of love, he quietly returned to his own house.

All this the skeptical outsider took in with growing

admiration. He stayed on in the village and became a disciple of the rabbi. Upon occasion, when he heard one of his fellow villagers saying that, "On Friday morning our rabbi ascends all the way to heaven", he would quietly add, "If not higher."[1]

Nobel laureate Saul Bellow has remarked that the survival of Jewish culture would have been inconceivable without the stories that gave point and purpose to the Jewish moral tradition. "If Not Higher" is a good example of a story that communicates a moral message that should be clear enough to understand on first reading. Unless, of course, one has no affection whatsoever for holiness. Instead of honoring the rabbi, one could chastise him for recklessly contributing to environmental ruin by his weekly assault on the community forest, for neglecting to place the old woman in a nursing home and her sick son in a hospital, or for encouraging the villagers' hagiographic attitude toward him as he calmly exploited their ignorance. Some would have preferred a hard-nosed social worker, a humanitarian scientist, an iconoclastic politician, or a liberal clergyman. But they would have missed the point. The story is simply saying, "Here is a good man. He is self-effacing and kind, merciful and humble. He is generous to the poor and compassionate toward the weak. We should want to be like this person. We should be more holy, because being holy is a beautiful way to be."

To see holiness where holiness exists is to be witness to a sacred reality. Franz Werfel, like Bellow and other writers in the Jewish tradition, was such a witness. Although he was among the millions of homeless during the German

---

[1] Christina Hoff Sommers, "Teaching the Virtues", *Imprimis,* November 1991, p. 4. The story Sommers relates is "If Not Higher", which appears in a collection of Jewish tales edited by Saul Bellow.

occupation of France in 1940, he still found reason, as he put it, "to magnify", even in an inhuman era, "the divine mystery and the holiness of man".[2]

Werfel had been an outspoken critic of the Nazis and was on their death list. In fact, the British radio had made the announcement, though erroneously, that Werfel had been murdered by the National Socialists. As fugitives, he and his wife found asylum in Lourdes, where nearly one hundred years before Mary, the Mother of God, had appeared to a peasant girl by the name of Bernadette Soubirous and identified herself as the "Immaculate Conception". The two remained in hiding in that historic city for several weeks. Each day they awakened wondering whether by sundown they would still be free or be prisoners condemned to death.

It was during this dreadful period that Werfel became acquainted with the story of the apparitions and the reports of the healings and favors that had occurred at Lourdes. One day while in great distress, he made a vow that if he escaped from his seemingly hopeless predicament and reached the saving shores of America, he would defer all other tasks and obligations and "sing" as best he could the "Song of Bernadette".

Werfel was faithful to his promise. *The Song of Bernadette* he wrote received great critical acclaim and became one of the most celebrated books of its time, remaining on the best-seller list of *The New York Times* for twenty-four weeks. It was translated into seven languages, and its 1943 movie version won four Academy Awards, including one for Jennifer Jones, who portrayed Bernadette. In writing *The*

[2] Franz Werfel, "A Personal Preface", in *The Song of Bernadette,* trans. Ludwig Lewisohn (Toronto: Macmillan, 1944) p. 7.

Song of Bernadette, Werfel did more than keep a promise. He continued the tradition of his people to proclaim the holiness of God by revealing the holiness of men.

Commentary

Holiness, as its etymology in almost every European language indicates, is a special form of wholeness. It differs from the common understanding of integrity in that it includes a unity with God. As such, it is man's conformity to the nature and will of God.

For Thomas Aquinas, holiness signifies two things. First, it denotes "purity", a meaning consistent with the Greek word for holiness, which means "unsoiled". In this regard, holiness implies a certain intimacy with God, because the human mind is frequently soiled in its contact with inferior things. Secondly, holiness denotes "firmness", because it demands an unswerving loyalty to God as man's first beginning and last end. In general, a person of holiness refers both himself and his actions to God and directs the acts of all other virtues to the divine good.[3]

Holiness is original. The holiness of God precedes all forms of unholiness, just as innocence comes before guilt, and as creation comes before the Fall. It is not reasonable, then, to remain unholy, because it is a rejection of one's original condition.

Because holiness is original, it is not ambitious. It consists, not in doing heroic or unusual things, but in doing everything with purity of heart.

[3] Thomas Aquinas, *Summa Theologiae,* II–II, 81, 8.

But not all height is holiness
Nor every sweetness good.[4]

Holiness imparts its splendor on its own, naturally, so to speak, and without fanfare. A lighthouse does not ring bells, send up flares, or shoot off cannons in order to communicate its presence—it just shines. Holiness is profoundly and effectively self-communicative. This is why Pascal exclaimed, "The serene, silent beauty of a holy life is the most powerful influence in the world, next to the might of the Spirit of God."

For Socrates, the primary source of holiness is the divine. In a conversation he has with an arrogant theologian, he poses one of the most important and fundamental questions that has ever emerged from the mouth of a philosopher: "Is what is holy holy because the gods approve it, or do they approve it because it is holy?"[5] His companion, who has unwittingly placed himself before the gods, does not grasp the rich implications of the question and eventually goes away unenlightened.

Socrates is directing our thought not only toward the absolute primacy of holiness but also to the notion that holiness is substantial and not the consequence of someone's approval. Therefore, the gods love holiness because it is holy. This accords holiness a position of priority, a ground beyond which one can go no farther. There is holiness, and holiness commands love, honor, and respect.

One of the most unfortunate features of the modern world is the dismissal of God and the enthronement of man

[4] Coventry Patmore, *Let Be.*
[5] Plato, *The Collected Dialogues,* E. Hamilton and H. Cairns (eds.), "Euthyphro" 10, trans. Lane Cooper (New York: Random House, 1966), p. 178.

in his place. By virtue of this usurpation, man becomes responsible for defining and generating his own holiness. "Love yourself through grace," wrote Nietzsche, "then you are no longer in need of your God, and you can act the whole drama of Fall and Redemption to its end in yourself."[6] With the eclipse of God and the decline of religion, it is no longer commonly believed that God is an eternal and unextinguishable source of wisdom and goodness, that God alone is the measure and the means of all holiness.

Holiness belongs primarily to God. Whatever degree of holiness an individual possesses does not originate within himself but through his intimacy with the Divine. Holiness is not an illusion; it is an objective reality apparent in the life of one who radiates the love of God.

[6] Friedrich Nietzsche, *Morgenröthe* (1881), no. 79.

HOPE

HOPE WAS THE motivating force that brought the Jewish ancestors of Mark and Elasah to America, specifically hope for a better life. The hope of Mark and Elasah, however, was of a different kind, not so much for a better life, but for something larger and less definable, something that would answer deeper yearnings.

Mark grew up in Los Angeles. His parents were proud of their heritage, but they were "cultural Jews" only. They greatly admired Marx, Freud, and Einstein, whom they regarded as a kind of trinity for all enlightened Jewish atheists. It was simply taken for granted that religion, as Marx held, was the "opiate of the people".

Mark's childhood was reasonably happy. He graduated from high school with honors and won a scholarship to a prestigious college. But he dropped out of college after a few months, depressed and confused. It was during that time in the mid-sixties that the counterrevolution was sweeping American campuses. Mark found himself caught up in the anti-establishment fervor and alienated from the accepted values of American culture. Material success no longer interested him. He began searching for something more meaningful, something to which he could commit his life. But he had no idea what this was, let alone how to achieve it. His immediate world offered him disillusionment, but not hope.

Elasah was born in a small midwestern town to Jewish parents who were rather lukewarm toward religion. When she was eight or nine years old, the thing she wanted most in the world was not another bike or some other toy but a baby brother or sister. That was the only thing she could remember wanting as a child and not getting. During the turmoil of the sixties, she left home and went to California, where everything she saw bewildered her. She eventually found herself, at age twenty-two, in Mexico having an abortion. At that point, she felt that life offered her nothing to hold onto. Her hopes and dreams seemed to have died with her unborn child. She was not sure whether she even wanted to live.

Mark and Elasah were both searching for something that would give their lives meaning and satisfy their deepest longings. The hippie movement eventually became passé, but the "straight world", with its unremitting emphasis on material success, still did not hold any appeal for them. Separately they learned about a new community in Northern California that was committed to doing "everything for the children". Believing that it would be here that they would find what they had been seeking, they became members. Within a year after meeting each other in this community, they were married. The wedding took place in 1969 in the Jewish Temple Elasah had attended as a child.

Although they had committed themselves to each other and to the children, they realized that something fundamental was still missing from their lives. Their search was not over. They did not suspect how much farther they would still have to travel. They read Scripture and gained an important measure of humility. A statement by C. S. Lewis expressed their frame of mind at this time: "At present we are on the outside of the world, the wrong side of the door.

We discern the freshness and purity of morning, but they do not make us fresh and pure. We cannot mingle with the splendors we see. But all the leaves of the New Testament are rustling with the rumor that it will not always be so. Some day, God willing, we shall get in."[1]

Because of their dedication to children, the members of the new community pledged themselves to work on behalf of the unborn. To their surprise, the only religious organization that supported their policy of "everything for the children" was the Catholic Church. Elasah soon entered the Church. Mark, however, did not and returned to his hometown of Los Angeles.

Mark deeply desired to return to his wife and family, but he knew that in order to do so, he would first have to become a Catholic. At the same time, he had the wisdom to know that if he did enter the Church, it had to be as a true believer. He knew, intuitively, that the Catholic faith is something that warrants respect.

One day, while in the church of Saint Teresa of Avila in downtown Los Angeles, Mark was profoundly and inexplicably moved by a statue of Mary. It was the image of a mother holding her child, one that silently communicated maternal kindness, protection, and help. He was moved even more by the inscription at the base of the statue. Although at the time he had no conscious understanding of what these words meant, he found them attractive, compelling, and a source of immense hope. He returned week after week to the statue and repeated, prayerfully, the words inscribed: "Into your hands do I place my eternal salvation, to you I entrust my soul." It took a long time

---

[1] C. S. Lewis, *Transposition and Other Addresses* (London: Geoffrey Bles, 1949), p. 31.

before he understood that he had consecrated himself, without realizing it, to Mary, the Mother of God.

The parish assistant at the church, a priest of ingratiating "ordinariness", instructed Mark in the faith and baptized him. Mark returned to his wife after a nine-month separation, and they were married in a Catholic ceremony in 1975. The following year they became Third Order Dominicans.[2]

Their community moved to New Hope, Kentucky, where Mark and Elasah continue their apostolate of providing help for the unborn and hope for women with distressed pregnancies.[3] On April 7, 1989, Mark and Elasah's tenth child was born. They named her Hope in honor of the virtue that has kept them on that steady, though convoluted course toward love and life.

Commentary

At the entrance of hell, inscribed in dim colors above the doorway's lofty arch, appeared a statement that caused Dante to shudder. Turning to his guide, the Roman poet Virgil, he said, "Master, these words import hard meaning." Hard meaning, indeed! "All hope abandon, ye who enter here" pronounce the very essence of hell—life without hope.[4] Shakespeare spoke about the wretched character who, after rejecting his own selfhood, falls into a living hell:

[2] Personal communication with Mark Drogin, March 3, 1995.

[3] Mark and Elasah Drogin, "Hope Is Worth a Billion Dollars an Ounce", in *The Ingrafting,* ed. Ronda Chervin (Petersham, Mass.: St. Bede's Publications, 1987), p. 54.

[4] Dante Alighieri, "Inferno", *The Divine Comedy,* trans. by Henry Francis Cary (New York: A. L. Burt, n.d.), canto 3, l. 9: "Lasciate ogni speranza, voi ch'enrate."

"And when he falls, he falls like Lucifer, / Never to hope again."[5]

To be without hope is to be in hell. People who exist without hope, whether they are dead or alive, exist in hell. We are, in the profoundest sense, creatures of hope. Not being able to hope is shattering to the soul and brings about unbearable torment.

Woody Allen once remarked that "marriage is the loss of hope." If he meant that marriage brings about the loss of vain and unprofitable illusions, he is correct. But disillusionment is not the same as the loss of hope. We often do not grasp real hope until its imposter has been dashed by disappointment. The disillusionment that often occurs within marriage is not the death of hope if through it the couple learns to accept the lack of perfection in each other and embraces the demands of true love.

Real hope is not crushed by disappointment. In fact, it is in difficulty that hope often is born. As Chesterton said, "As long as matters are really hopeful, hope is a mere flattery or platitude; it is when everything is hopeless that hope begins to be a strength at all. Like all the Christian virtues, it is as unreasonable as it is indispensable."[6]

A person's "hopes" are capable of obscuring his one hope. When his small hopes fail to materialize, one by one, he runs the risk of forgetting what is most important and falls into despair. Thus we can read in the newspaper of an athlete who committed suicide because the National Basketball Association did not draft him, or about a gambler who resorted to violence because he lost a sizable bet, or an actress who became acutely depressed when she failed to

[5] William Shakespeare, *Henry VIII,* 3.2.371.
[6] G. K. Chesterton, *Heretics* (London: John Lane, 1952), p. 119.

land a leading role. In the movie version of Katherine Anne Porter's *Ship of Fools,* a broken-down, chronic alcoholic explains to a sober and well-adjusted midget that he turned to drink for no other reason than his inability to hit the curveball.

We easily attach ourselves to trivial hopes. We hope the weather is good for the picnic, or that our team will win the important game, or that we will win the lottery. All these hopes are subservient to the one fundamental hope, namely, that our being will one day be fulfilled. This is our far-flung hope, the one, as Keats remarks, that exists "beyond the shadow of a dream".

We just as easily attach ourselves to vain hopes that are mounted on the slippery slope of pride. And just as pride precedes a fall, vain hopes prepare the same unhappy fate:

> This is the state of man: to-day he puts forth
> The tender leaves of hopes; tomorrow blossoms,
> And bears his blushing honours thick upon him;
> The third day comes a frost, a killing frost,
> And, when he thinks, good easy man, full surely
> His greatness is a-ripening, nips his root,
> And then he falls . . . [7]

We need difficulties to enliven our hope, patience to test it, a community to support it, and God to direct it. We purify our hope as we separate what is superficial from what is essential, what is fleeting from what is lasting. As Herman Melville has said, "Hope proves man deathless. It is the struggle of the soul, breaking loose from what is perishable and attesting her eternity."

Perspective is important in understanding hope. There

---

[7] William Shakespeare, *Henry VIII,* 3.2.371.

are tides of hope that change with our changing stages of life. Emerson writes of the rising and setting of this hope in a most poetic and compassionate way: "Hope writes the poetry of the boy, but memory that of the man. Man looks forward with smiles, but backward with sighs. Such is the wise providence of God. The cup of life is sweetness at the brim—the flavor is impaired as we drink deeper, and the dregs are made bitter that we may not struggle when it is taken from our lips."

Ultimate hope transcends all other hopes. It is the hope that transcends our earthly life. Because we are always unfinished and unfulfilled, we are constantly hoping for a better state. This hope does not expire with age. The Christian tradition regards man as a "pilgrim", a "wayfarer", *Homo Viator.* It views him as having his ultimate hope in God. This is why Kierkegaard equates despair with the loss of the eternal. The loss of the earthly, he contends, cannot be the cause of despair. Those things that are within easy reach, what he identifies collectively as "immediacy", are able to distract a person and render him unaware of the eternal. When a person fails to gain something that is very important to him, he may think he has cause for despair. However, as Kierkegaard argues, such a person has already despaired, specifically, at the time he lost sight of his relationship with the eternal. "It is as if one were to stand with one's back toward the City Hall and the Court House, and, pointing straight before him, were to say, 'There is the City Hall and the Court House.' The man is right, there it is . . . if he turns around."[8] The loss of hope—despair—is ultimately the refusal to be oneself and to accept one's

[8] Søren Kierkegaard, *The Sickness unto Death,* trans. Walter Lowrie (Garden City, N.Y.: Doubleday, 1954), p. 185.

destiny. It is a preference for immediacies and illusions over authenticity and eternity. To renew one's fundamental hope, one must "turn around" and face what is most real and most important and embrace it with one's whole being.

HUMILITY

Karl August Rudolph Steinmetz was born in Breslau, Germany, in 1865. He was born with a severe curvature of the spine. When he grew to manhood, he was barely five feet tall and hunched over. His mother died when he was a year old, and he was reared by his Polish grandmother in his native city.

At the University of Breslau, he exhibited such a marvelous facility of moving from one intellectual field of inquiry to another that students called him "Proteus" after the mythical figure who could instantly assume the shape of another being. Steinmetz had fulfilled all the requirements for his doctoral degree. His dissertation had been accepted. All that remained was the formality of confirming the degree. But he never obtained it. While editor of an illegal socialist newspaper, he had attracted the attention of the authorities, who were zealous in their enforcement of anti-socialist laws promulgated by Prime Minister Otto von Bismarck. Steinmetz was forced to flee the country.

After spending a year in Switzerland, a sympathetic colleague offered to pay his way to the United States. Steinmetz and his colleague arrived in New York on June 1, 1889, in the steerage section of a French liner. Immigration authorities were reluctant to admit Steinmetz into the country. His distorted body, poverty, and

113

lack of friends led officials to believe that he was likely to become a "public charge". Through the intervention of his traveling companion, who assured the officials that he would look after his friend, Steinmetz was finally allowed to enter the country. At that time, Steinmetz had ten dollars, had no job prospects, and could speak no English.

By 1892, Steinmetz had established a reputation for himself in the world of science. He formulated the law of histeresis, by which one can determine the power that is lost in electrical devices when magnetic action is converted into unusable heat. The application of this knowledge greatly improved the design of electrical machines. He was soon invited to join the newly formed General Electric Company, where he spent the remainder of his career in research on electricity.

Steinmetz is best known for his development of the theory of alternating currents and for his experiments with "man-made lightning". He also calculated a way of harnessing the power of the mighty Niagara. A total of 195 patents were registered in his name. Perhaps his most ironic contribution to society, in the light of his condition as a diminutive hunchback, was an improved electric motor for the Otis Elevator Company, which thereby made skyscrapers a practical reality.

Despite the spectacular contributions he made to science and their immense potential benefit for society, he remained throughout his life a man of striking humility. One contemporary observer wrote that the briefest contact with Steinmetz "reveals a singular individuality and that of a very high order, a man of fine and ready mind and one crammed full of passion for work . . . , an individuality which combines authority in utterance with a remarkably childlike personal humility".[1]

Behind the red-brick house where Steinmetz lived, in Schenectady, New York, was the scientist's laboratory and a glass conservatory where he grew orchids and other exotic plants. But his favorite flower, the one with which he identified, was the humble cactus. "Cacti may be ugly and deformed," he explained, "but they can live and flourish, producing flowers of great beauty under the worst possible conditions."[2] For Steinmetz, the great underlying principle of all human progress is that "divine discontent" that makes men strive for better conditions.[3]

Contentment never played much part in the life of Steinmetz. Although General Electric provided him with an expensive leather chair, he seldom used it. Because of his deformity, he preferred to kneel on a chair or stool whenever he worked. The posture spoke eloquently of his spirit. The floor of his laboratory was never waxed because of the danger that he might slip and injure himself.

Steinmetz never married, though he did legally adopt a son and became a foster grandfather to his adopted son's three children. He championed educational opportunities for handicapped children, establishing special classes for

[1] Joseph Baker, *Scientific American,* May 6, 1911.

[2] Sigmund Lavine, *Steinmetz, Maker of Lightning,* p. 101. See also John Winthrop Hammond, *Charles Proteus Steinmetz* (New York: Century, 1924), pp. 261–62: "[Steinmetz] brought together a collection of cacti that was said to rank second only to the collection in the Kew Gardens in England. The specimens included scores and even hundreds of the ungainly euphorbia, the old-man cactus, the fishhook and hedgehog species, the aloe, the agave, and the columnar cactus."

[3] *American Magazine,* May 1918.

those who were subnormal, tubercular, or anemic. He was a tireless advocate for bettering the living conditions of the underprivileged.

He died at age fifty-eight, following a strenuous trip to the Pacific Coast. The medical examiners reported that he died of acute dilation of the heart, following a chronic myocarditis of many years' standing. The room in the Steinmetz house where his body lay in state was filled with flowers. For four hours unbroken lines of people filed past his bier. Among those who paid their last respects, in addition to many dignitaries, were groups of children.[4] It was fitting that at the very end, the mighty and the humble whom he had embraced throughout his life returned to embrace him.

Commentary

Given the finite condition of man and his checkered history, one might think that humility, a human virtue of such evident appropriateness, would be easy to appropriate. It should be the first lesson we learn from self-reflection! Nonetheless, despite how well-tailored humility is to suit men, its correlative vice—pride—is what they are more likely to display. Rather than bow to reality and accept themselves as they are, men are far more likely to cherish illusions and pretend to be what they are not. As one pundit remarked, "Many would be scantily clad if clothed in their humility."

The humble person makes a realistic assessment of who he is and puts that unillusioned judgment into practice. He

---

[4] Sender Garlin, *Charles P. Steinmetz: Scientist and Socialist* (New York: AIMS, 1977), p. 25.

does not judge himself to be smaller or larger than he really is. In so doing he avoids despair as well as pride. Consequently, the humble person enjoys the freedom to be who he is. He is not troubled by accidentals, such as reputation, self-interest, or failure. He takes joy in the importance or excellence of what is done rather than in the incidental fact that he happened to be the one who did it. As for illusions, which often consume huge amounts of time and energy, he has none to defend. He is not troubled by feeling obliged to defend an imaginary self to people who do not know who he really is. Nor does he expect others to be who they are not. He has no concern for trading in unrealities. He is not a candidate for being victimized by self-pity. He is not likely to be saddened by not being who he cannot be. Because of the priceless freedom to be who a person truly is, Thomas Merton can say that "the beginning of humility is the beginning of blessedness and the consummation of humility is the perfection of all joy."[5] For Confucius, "Humility is the solid foundation of all the virtues."

The great mathematician-physicist Albert Einstein confessed that he was troubled by the adulation he received. He felt it was grossly disproportionate to his own more humble and realistic estimate of himself. "There are plenty of the well-endowed, thank God", wrote the author of the theory of relativity. "It strikes me as unfair, and even in bad taste, to select a few of them for boundless admiration, attributing superhuman powers of mind and character to them. This has been my fate, and the contrast between the popular estimate of my powers and achievements and the reality is simply grotesque."

A philosopher, who understood the fundamental impor-

<hr />

[5] Thomas Merton, *Seeds of Contemplation* (New York: Dell Publishing, 1949), p. 103.

tance of humility in the broad scheme of things, was once asked what the great God was doing. He replied: "His whole employment is to lift up the humble and cast down the proud." Since humility is fruitful and pride self-destructive, such an employment would be perfectly consistent with God's love for his creatures.

Jascha Heifetz and Mischa Elman, both preeminent violinists, were dining together in a restaurant when a waiter presented them with an envelope addressed to "The World's Greatest Violinist". Since the two were good friends and held each other's artistry in the highest esteem, neither wanted to assume the letter was addressed to himself. When Heifetz begged Elman to open the envelope, the latter bowed and deferred to the former. When Elman insisted the letter must be for his companion, Heifetz, likewise, demurred to his partner. Finally, Elman's persistence was persuasive, and Heifetz reluctantly opened the letter and read the salutation: "Dear Fritz" (their illustrious colleague Fritz Kreisler).[6]

It is easy to imagine the two violinists being humbled by the incident. By contrast, Socrates interpreted the oracle's statement, "No man is wiser than Socrates", with rare humility. The "gadfly" of Athens correctly took it to mean that no man is wise. "Humility", as Cardinal Newman once explained, "is one of the most difficult of virtues both to attain and to ascertain. It lies close upon the heart itself, and its tests are exceedingly delicate and subtle."[7]

Among philosophers, Socrates is perhaps best associated

[6] Edmund Fuller, ed., *Thesaurus of Anecdotes* (New York: Crown Publishers, 1942), p. 241.

[7] John Henry Cardinal Newman, *The Idea of a University* (Garden City, N.Y.: 1959), p. 214.

with the virtue of humility. Because he knew he did not possess wisdom, he was constantly in pursuit of it. Hence, his life-long search for a master-teacher. Yet his humility proved to be a great asset inasmuch as it freed him from the distorting influence of pride. He saw the human condition with exceptional clarity, so much so that he earned the distinction of being the "Father of Moral Philosophy".

"Humility", states Henry David Thoreau, "like darkness reveals the heavenly lights."[8] All genuine appreciation of things requires seeing them against a boundary of nonexistence. From the perspective of nonbeing, all light seems lightning, every sensation becomes sensational, and each phenomenon appears to be phenomenal. The attitude of humility, because it expects nothing, is ready to appreciate everything. The person who empties himself is best prepared to fill himself with the wonders of the universe. As G. K. Chesterton has pointed out, "It is one of the million wild jests of truth that we know nothing until we know nothing."[9]

On a more theological level, Saint Augustine maintains that humility is the first, second, and third most important factor in religion. It is, in his judgment, the foundation of all other virtues. Consequently, there can be no virtue in the soul in which humility is lacking, only the appearance of virtue.

Even the devil may clothe himself in the appearance of virtue. When Saint Macarius once returned to his cell, he met the devil, who tried to cut him in half with a sickle. The devil failed in repeated attempts, because when he

---

[8] Henry David Thoreau, "Walden", in *The American Tradition in Literature,* vol. 1 (New York: W. W. Norton, 1957), p. 963.

[9] G. K. Chesterton, *Orthodoxy* (Garden City, N.Y.: Doubleday, 1957), p. 32.

drew near the saint, he lost his energy. Then, full of anger, he said: "I suffer great violence from you, Macarius, because though I greatly desire to harm you, I cannot. I do all that you do and more. You fast once in a while, I never eat. You sleep little, I never close my eyes. You are chaste, and so am I. In one thing only do you surpass me." "And what is this thing?" asked Macarius. He answered: "It is your great humility." And with that, the devil disappeared.[10]

Canadian artist Michael O'Brien dedicated a year of his work to illustrating the fifteen mysteries of the Rosary. When he came to the "Assumption of Mary into Heaven", he found himself devoid of any inner suggestion as to how he might depict this particular mystery. In fact, he was so barren of artistic ideas that he even thought of omitting it from the series. It was at that time that he happened to read a passage in Thomas Aquinas that stated that God sends an angel to assist people in completing a work that glorifies God. Encouraged by this passage, O'Brien prayed for an assisting angel. Then it all came to him. He suddenly knew, without any accompanying emotion, exactly what colors, shapes, figures, and design he must use in executing the painting. As he himself readily admits, "What was to have been my most difficult painting was the easiest one I ever painted in my life."[11] The painting is actually the most captivating of the series and adorns the cover of the published edition of these illustrated mysteries.[12]

Humility is the mother of many virtues, because from it

[10] *Spiritual Diary: Selected Sayings and Examples of Saints* (Boston: St. Paul Books and Media, 1990), p. 37.

[11] Personal communication with the artist, January 5, 1995.

[12] Michael O'Brien, *The Mysteries of the Rosary* (Ottawa: The White Horse Press, 1992).

knowledge, realism, honesty, strength, and dedication are born. "Humility, that low, sweet root," writes the poet Thomas Moore, "From which all heavenly virtues shoot."[13]

[13] Thomas Moore, *Loves of the Angels: Third Angel's Story.*

INTEGRITY

THE JARDIN DES PLANTES is a charming park in Paris that is especially dear to Parisians of the Left Bank. One may spend a casual afternoon there, strolling amidst the exotic trees, browsing at the museum of natural history, enjoying the animals in the zoo, observing the glow of young lovers, or simply taking delight in the knowledge that one is alive and free—at least for the moment—from the anxieties of a deeply troubled world.

Jacques Maritain and his girlfriend Raïssa Oumansoff went there often and invariably found it both enchanting and relaxing. One day, however, while walking through the Jardin des Plantes, a different mood possessed them. The two had been at the Sorbonne for a few years and were discussing the effect that their study had had on them. It was a dour review that left them more than unhappy. The relativism of the scientists and the skepticism of the philosophers produced in them a "deep distress of heart" that they could hardly bear.[1]

Jacques had no particular religious convictions, while Raïssa judged herself to be an atheist. The metaphysical anguish they felt that day would prove difficult to describe. Many years later, when Raïssa wrote about it in her memoirs, she said: "It is true that I have had other sufferings, other

[1] Raïssa Maritain, *We Have Been Friends Together,* trans. Julie Kernan (Garden City, N.Y.: Doubleday, 1961), p. 65.

sorrows, often great sorrow, but this particular distress I have never since known. Nevertheless I have not forgotten it. One does not forget the gates of death."[2]

What was it that so troubled them? It was an almost unconscious dignity of the mind that rebelled—powerfully and painfully—at the thought that there is no light by which any meaning for human existence can be found. They thoroughly abhorred the "pseudointelligence" that was capable of knowing everything else but truth. What purpose did philosophy serve if it had neither love nor wisdom—and if it had nothing to do with life? It is one thing to live an unhappy life. That is bearable. But to live an absurd life is an unbearable affront to our deeper need for meaning.

They considered and immediately rejected the prospect of living a life of prejudice and dissimulation, of guessing at the meaning of existence or pretending that it does not matter. They could be neither superficial nor hypocritical. An inner sense of personal integrity demanded with compelling force that each be one in mind and heart, in thought and action, in who they were and in what could give them a sense of pride.

They both came to the conclusion that life in the pale, shadowy light of relativism and skepticism was not worth living. So they agreed to an experiment. They would do everything they could over the course of the following year to discover a means by which truth could be known. If they failed in their endeavor, they would commit suicide. "We wanted to die by a free act", Raïssa records, "if it were impossible to live according to truth."[3] They preferred to

---

[2] Ibid., p. 66.
[3] Ibid., p. 68.

die with integrity rather than go on living, and thereby endorsing, an existence that would be vain and pointless. As Raïssa goes on to say, "we could extend credit to existence, look upon it as an experiment to be made, in the hope that to our ardent plea, the meaning of life would reveal itself, that new values would stand forth so clearly that they would enlist our total allegiance, and deliver us from the nightmare of a useless and sinister world."[4]

It was then, as Raïssa recalls, that God's pity led them to Henri Bergson. It was through Bergson's philosophy and lectures at the College of France that Jacques and Raïssa found the light of intelligence they had been seeking. Bergson explained to them how the human mind is capable of grasping what is real through an act of intuition. This was the beginning of the answer the two young students had been seeking. The credit they had extended to existence continued to pay rich dividends. Jacques and Raïssa were married in a civil ceremony in 1904. Subsequently, they met a series of illustrious friends, especially Léon Bloy, who called himself a "Pilgrim of the Absolute". Through the inspiration of the thought and the example of the lives of these friends, Jacques and Raïssa were led to an acceptance of Catholicism. They were baptized on June 11, 1906, with Bloy and his wife serving as godparents.

Three years later, Raïssa introduced her husband to the *Summa Theologiae* of Saint Thomas Aquinas. His response was immediate and passionate. Although Bergson had enabled the Maritains to overcome scientistic relativism and philosophical skepticism, it was Aquinas who carried them much farther in their intellectual quest. Their lifelong

[4] Ibid.

course was set. Jacques, with the help of his wife, became the twentieth century's foremost proponent of the thought of Saint Thomas. He wrote more than fifty philosophical works. Pope Paul VI referred to him as "my teacher" and "*un santo*". One author appraised him as "the most beautiful example I know of intellectual charity in our century".[5] Raïssa, in addition to her poetry and her two-volume memoir, wrote other works, including a life of Thomas Aquinas. After she died in 1960, Jacques entered the community of the Little Brothers of Jesus in Toulouse, France. There he confided to a friend that without Raïssa he could be brave but not happy in this life. He took vows in 1961 and passed away four years later at ninety-one years of age.

Commentary

Courage is the virtue that prevents a person from going to pieces. Integrity keeps him from breaking into fragments. The Maritains strove for an integration of their outer life with their inner convictions. They were driven by an unrelenting desire for a unified personality.

The wholeness of a person is subject to disintegration, that is, decomposition into mutually exclusive parts. Head and heart, reality and image, private self and public persona are often at odds with each other. Specialization and bureaucracy contribute heavily to this process of disintegration. Politics is another area that poses a formidable challenge to anyone who wants to retain his integrity. On

---

[5] Henry Bars quoted in "Two Souls", *Catholic World Report*, February 1992, p. 51.

the abortion issue, for example, one commonly hears about politicians who are privately opposed but publicly in favor of it.

The threats to personal integrity are virtually everywhere. Kurt Vonnegut, in his novel *Mother Night,* writes about the schizophrenia that was rampant under National Socialism in Nazi Germany. A typical citizen of that era was a good family man at home and a dedicated promoter of global aggression at work. George Orwell's concept of "double-think" outlines how a totalitarian regime is better able to control people if the citizens themselves have no understanding of or appreciation for personal integrity.

Ignazio Silone writes about a judge who separated his professional self from his personal self so thoroughly that he could find a poor seamstress guilty of provoking the dog that mauled her. Although he knew the injured woman was innocent, he made no effort to bring the facts of the case to light. Not wanting his personal knowledge to influence his professional duty, he allowed the woman's defense to proceed so poorly that the evidence and testimony admitted in the case compelled him to render a decision he knew to be unjust.[6]

In the January 7 issue of *The Financial Post,* Erik Larson writes about a publishing house that publishes books instructing readers on such subjects as how to make bombs and how to kill people. These books are well known to police and federal agents who have found them in the libraries of serial killers and bombers. The publisher's catalogue includes such titles as: 21 *Techniques of Silent Killing; Hit Man: A Technical Manual for Independent Contractors;* and

[6] *The God That Failed,* ed. Richard Crossman (New York: Bantam Books, 1965), p. 74.

Homemade C–4, a guide to making powerful explosions. The moral defense the owner of the publishing house offers in justifying these works is a model of personal self-fragmentation. "As a human," he says, "I feel very sorry for anyone who's put through any physical suffering. As a publisher and as a pragmatist, I feel absolutely no responsibility for the misuse [*sic*] of information."[7]

The primary danger the self-divided person faces is the possibility of not knowing who he is. Kierkegaard offers a parable that illuminates this point. A certain peasant made enough money to regale himself in expensive finery. On his way home, in a drunken state, he lay down in the middle of the road and fell asleep. An approaching wagon awakened him, but when he looked at his legs that he was not accustomed to see so well-attired, he said to the driver, "Drive on, they are not my legs."[8] On this same subject, Nathaniel Hawthorne has remarked that "No man can, for any considerable time, wear one face to himself, and another to the multitude, without finally getting bewildered as to which is the true one."

A favorite theme among existential philosophers and writers is the fundamental moral importance of personal integrity. The word they often use to describe this state is "authenticity". A person should be himself, they insist, and not divide himself into incompatible parts: one for himself and another for the masses.

Cowardice may be a factor in causing a person to lose integrity. His fear of public opinion or what his boss might think could lead him to make a false presentation of who he

[7] Erik Larson, "Publisher Makes a Killing with How-To Violence Books", *The Financial Post,* January 7, 1994, p. 9.

[8] Søren Kierkegaard, *The Sickness unto Death,* trans. by Walter Lowrie (Garden City, N.Y.: Doubleday, 1954), p. 187.

knows himself to be. He is therefore one thing to himself and something different to those he fears. This is what existentialists usually have in mind when they speak of inauthenticity. Paul Tillich's classic *The Courage to Be* discusses the fundamental importance of maintaining personal authenticity by standing firm—not surrendering one's integrity—at times when it is so tempting to be less than whole.

Pride may be a factor when a person tries to create the impression that he is better than he really is. This vice is commonly called hypocrisy. The hypocrite usually has modest aims and is content merely to have people think of him in flattering terms. He is less harmful than the seducer who pretends he is good so that he can lure people into harm. The seducer represents the added vice of malice. The devil is the archetypal model of an iniquitous heart concealed by sheep's clothing:

> The devil can cite Scripture
>   for his purpose.
> An evil soul producing holy
>   witness
> Is like a villain with a smiling
>   cheek,
> A goodly apple rotten at the
>   heart;
> O what a goodly outside
>   falsehood hath![9]

The devil is a creature of nonintegrity, par excellence. He is a multiplicity. This is why Scripture refers to him as "legion". And because he once lived in heaven, he knows how to appear to be better than he is. Personal inauthenticity

---

[9] William Shakespeare, *The Merchant of Venice*, 3.3.99.

that results from a disregard of integrity weakens us and makes us vulnerable to the devil's enticements. Integrity, though it may not win the plaudits of others, puts us on a path that leads to God. Integrity is a natural wholeness that opens the door to supernatural holiness.

JUSTICE

WHAT AN AUTHOR WRITES and what he experiences are mysteriously interwoven. Fyodor Dostoevsky's *Crime and Punishment,* his most popular work, is unimaginable apart from his own experiences of moral transgressions and the spiritual need for punishment they set in motion. He could not have drawn the compelling characters that appear in the novel had he not been subject to indelibly powerful moral experiences himself.

Dostoevsky wrote his first novel, *Poor Folk,* when he was twenty-four. It immediately became the rage of all Russia. Several short stories soon followed, which confirmed his earlier critics' prediction of his greatness as a writer. This first part of his literary career was brought to an abrupt end, however, when the Czarist government moved in on a revolutionary group Dostoevsky had been rash enough to join, though more out of youthful innocence than any genuinely revolutionary conviction. As harmless as his participation in this group may have been, Dostoevsky was condemned to death along with his companions. The Czar, in a cruel hoax, allowed all the preparations for the execution to be carried out except for the final shots of the firing squad. At the last moment the Czar's commutation arrived, but the psychological effect on Dostoevsky and his comrades left its mark. One of the men went insane. Dostoevsky portrayed this unfortunate individual in his novel *The Idiot.*

After the mock execution, Dostoevsky served a four-year term in an inhuman, forced-labor camp in Siberia. That was followed by five years as a common soldier in the semibarbaric outposts of the Czar's empire. These experiences, torturous as they were, were not without value. They allowed Dostoevsky to gain profound insights into the minds of thieves and murderers. Also, the teachings of Christ and the spirituality of the Russian Orthodox Church took on a deeper meaning for him and helped him to understand the relationship between suffering and salvation.

Crime and Punishment is the masterpiece of Dostoevsky's second literary period. The story centers on an impoverished student, Raskolnikov (the Russian word for "divided" or "schizophrenic"), who is infected by the rationalistic nihilism of his young revolutionary-minded generation. Raskolnikov believes the human race to be composed of "losers" and "winners", the former being the submissive type who need to be ruled by conventional moral law, the latter being supermen who are above the moral law. Fancying himself to be a member of the elite group, he commits murder to prove to himself that he is indeed above the law and can kill another human being without arousing any pangs of conscience. He believes he can justify his act solely on the basis of his presumed superiority. He kills an old pawnbroker and her stepsister. He rationalizes that he has put them out of their misery while providing himself with the money he needs to further his education and to mitigate the poverty of his mother and his sister.

His experiment in murder backfires. His guilt is insuppressible. Soon after his crime, he is stricken with a high fever that lasts for four days. During this time authorities visit him in his room and hear him say things in the fever-induced delirium that establish him as a suspect. Raskolnikov is tormented by his guilt and eventually confesses to the prostitute Sonya. "But I only killed a louse, Sonya—foul, useless, pernicious." Sonya is not taken in: "A human being a louse!" Raskolnikov becomes more candid: "I decided to kill someone, to kill without casuistry, for myself, for myself alone! . . . I had to know then and as soon as possible whether I was a louse like all the rest, or a man. Could I step over, or couldn't I? Dare I bend down and take it or not? Am I a trembling cur, or have I the *right*—." Sonya urges him to confess his crime because she knows that only then will God send him life again.[1]

Raskolnikov had tried to divorce his reason from the claims of the heart, or according to one critic, he tried to substitute reason for life.[2] But his experience had been a complete failure. He could not justify his crime, no matter how ingenious his rationalizations. He discovered, instead, an inescapable basis for ultimate justice within his own being. The law of justice imbedded within himself cried out for punishment. He could not be whole again unless he confessed his crime and accepted his punishment.

Raskolnikov made his confession and served an eight-year prison sentence in Siberia. Sonya stayed in a village near the prison camp so that she could visit him. Through her love he began his regeneration. Life took the place of dialectics, and, like Lazarus, he slowly came back from the dead. As Dostoevsky said of Raskolnikov and Sonya: "The heart of one held infinite sources of life for the heart of the other."[3]

[1] Fyodor Dostoevsky, *Crime and Punishment,* trans. by Michael Scammell (New York: Washington Square Press, 1969), pp. 433–36.

[2] Joanne G. Kashdan, "Crime and Punishment", *Masterplots,* ed. Frank N. Magill (Englewood Cliffs, N.J.: Salem Press, 1976), p. 1,200.

[3] Ibid., p. 573.

Before *Crime and Punishment* was published, Dostoevsky had written his publisher that his novel would be the psychological telling of a crime committed by a young student who "had submitted to certain 'incomplete' ideas which float on the wind". He added that in this work he would develop the theme "that the legal punishment inflicted for a crime intimidates a criminal infinitely less than law-makers suppose, in part because the criminal himself *morally demands punishment*".[4]

Justice is profoundly personal. A sin against one's neighbor is an injustice that claims two victims, both the neighbor and the perpetrator. Moral decisions must not be based solely on cold, self-interested rationality. The presence of the other stops us and demands that we be just. The law of justice transcends us, but our inner spiritual reality demands we conform to it. "What the law requires" is written on our hearts, says Saint Paul. When we try to erase it, we destroy not only our neighbor but our very selves. The light of justice shines, therefore, only once the circuitry between self and neighbor is complete.

"Justice is directed toward the other person", writes Thomas Aquinas ("Justitia est ad alterum"). This simple statement is rich in implication. The individual who is wholly absorbed in himself, like Raskolnikov before his conversion, is unable to be just to anyone. A world populated by such people is completely devoid of justice. Justice begins only at the moment people begin thinking about what they owe others.

In a world of injustice, people are lonely and fearful; in a world of justice, they are communal and trusting. The immoderate self-interest of the unjust individual deprives

---

[4] Ibid., introduction, p. xiii.

him of all social support. It is a form of self-interest that is perfectly inimical to what is truly in his best interest. The unjust individual desocializes himself. He becomes a fugitive from humanity. In doing as he pleases, he may think he is benefiting himself, but, in actuality, he is alienating himself from the very center of his own personhood, that greater self by which he is morally bound to all others.

Although we are bound to our neighbor by invisible cords of justice, we are not likely to render him justice if we do not have the least regard for him in the first place. Justice, therefore, presupposes love. In the absence of love, it is merely an equation, a mathematical abstraction. We cannot love everyone passionately, but we can love everyone justly, even strangers. Justice is the rectitude of our love that we owe all men. Nonetheless, exercising justice without love is only too commonplace.

Victor Hugo tells a story that illustrates this separation of justice from love. Having exhausted his means, an unhappy man, through love for a woman and for the child she had borne him, took to making counterfeit money. At that time counterfeiting was punishable by death. The woman was arrested for passing the first copies he made. She refused to testify against him and vehemently denied his guilt. The procurator of the king (*procurateur du roi*), however, devised a shrewd plan. By means of skillfully piecing together fragments of letters, he succeeded in persuading the unfortunate woman that she had a rival and that her man had been unfaithful to her. Moved by jealousy, she denounced her lover, confessed all, and supplied the needed proof of his guilt.

When the story circulated, everybody was in awe of the adroitness of the procurator. It was indeed clever of him to bring jealousy into play, they thought, and bring the truth to light by means of anger and revenge. Upon hearing the story and learning the location of the upcoming trial, a certain clergyman who had a reputation for holiness took a different view of the officer's strategy. He asked, softly, "And where is the *procurateur du roi* to be tried?"[5]

The clergyman could plainly see the woman had been unjustly manipulated. The official had used deception as a way of inciting desires for revenge and extracting a confession. And he used the woman as a mere means to an end. "Justice is the virtue that gives each his due", as Augustine tells us.[6] Justice presupposes rights. If something is owed to another, it is only because that other person has a prior right to it. The counterfeiter's mistress had a right not to be lied to and emotionally manipulated. She had a right not to be used as a tool. Pascal wisely noted that justice and power require a proper balance with each other. "Justice and power must be brought together", he wrote, so that "what is just is strong, and what is strong is just."[7]

Justice is personal in the sense that it is anchored in a concern for the person and that person's rights. At the same time, it is impersonal inasmuch as true justice is neither the plaything of the powerful nor the convenience of the vulnerable. Accordingly, Aquinas cites two main reasons for men falling short of justice: "deference to magnates, deference to the mob".[8]

There are three fundamental forms of justice. The first is

[5] Victor Hugo, *Les Misérables,* trans. Charles E. Wilbour (New York: Modern Library, 1990), pp. 13–14.

[6] Augustine, *The Free Choice of the Will,* trans. Francis E. Tourscher (Philadelphia: Peter Reilly, 1937), p. 67.

[7] Pascal, *Pensées,* trans. Martin Turnell (New York: Harper and Row, 1962), p. 88.

[8] Thomas Aquinas, *Commentary on Job,* 34, lect. 2.

the justice that individuals owe each other. This is the order that the parts of society have to each other and is called *commutative* justice. The second form of justice describes the relationship between the whole and its parts, or the social whole to individuals. This form of justice is *distributive.* Lastly, there is the order of the parts to the whole, which is called *legal* or *general* justice.

Each of these forms of justice has some kind of indebtedness in common with the others. In commutative justice, individuals should return whatever they owe to each other. The protection the state owes its citizens exemplifies distributive justice. The obligation to pay the government taxes one owes is an example of legal justice.

In concert, these three types of justice form the ligaments that hold civilized beings together within a civilized community. They embody the Golden Rule and honor the principle that all men are, as human beings, equal in nature and equal in the eyes of the law.

LOYALTY

HE WAS A MAN of refined and diverse abilities. His eloquence in Latin, as well as in English, was incomparable, and he had mastered Greek. He was an imaginative writer, a poet, a musician, a translator, a lecturer, and a lawyer of exceptional quality. During his illustrious political career he was Speaker of the House of Commons and Lord Chancellor of England. But Sir Thomas More is remembered and honored more for his virtues than for his virtuosity, particularly for the loyalty he held to his God and his Church when his life was on the line.

Samuel Johnson said of him that "he was the person of the greatest virtue these islands ever produced."[1] Joseph Addison stated that "his death was a piece with his life. . . . He did not look upon the severing of his head from his body as a circumstance that ought to produce any change in the disposition of his mind."[2]

When More was a member of Parliament, early in his career, he brashly and successfully opposed the large and unjust sums of money that King Henry VII was exacting from his subjects. It was an act that previewed things to come. More was later informed by one of the king's tax collectors that he would have lost his head except for the

---

[1] Quoted in Robert Bolt, *A Man for All Seasons* (Scarborough, Ont.: Bellhaven House, 1968), p. ii.

[2] Joseph Addison, *The Spectator,* no. 349.

fact that he had not attacked the king in person. He remained conscious of the possibility of losing his head while he served King Henry VIII, even during that period when his relationship with the Crown was most cordial. "If my head should win him a castle in France," he told Roper, his son-in-law and biographer, "it should not fail to go."[3]

More was an adept diplomat and never went out of his way to invite trouble. When Henry VIII declared himself the Supreme Head of the Church of England, More proffered his resignation. But Henry was determined to obtain More's allegiance and issued the Act of Succession that required all who should be called to take an oath that honored Henry's marriage to Anne Boleyn and repudiated the papacy. When More was summoned by the king to take the oath, he refused. More was then charged with treason and sent to prison. He was executed the following year.

Robert Bolt, who wrote the immensely successful play about Thomas More *A Man for All Seasons,* asks himself the question: "Why do I take for my hero a man who brings about his own death because he can't put his hand on an old black book and tell an ordinary lie?"[4] His answer, essentially, is that the virtue that More lives (and dies) by, his loyalty to his primary commitment, is a testimony that he has a self, an inner personal reality that cannot be denied or swept aside by fears or inducements. More proves he is a self because he stands by his word. The vacillating, back-tracking individual who switches loyalties whenever it is convenient does not reveal the presence of a self. Such a person seems to be indistinguishable from the external forces that mold him. Perhaps it is the case that one's clear

[3] William Roper, *The Life of Sir Thomas More,* in Thomas More, *Utopia* (Princeton, N.J.: Van Nostrand, 1947), p. 223.

[4] Bolt, p. xiii.

sense of self can crystallize only in conjunction with something transcendent, that is, something real that does not suffer from the metaphysical infirmity of finitude and transitoriness.

More cannot be loyal to his king if it requires that he not be loyal to himself. This is why Bolt has his character say: "I neither could nor would rule the King. But there's a little . . . little area . . . where I must rule myself. It's very little—less to him than a tennis court."[5]

King Henry had required More to swear loyalty to him. But More knew this meant swearing disloyalty to God and Rome. It was bad enough for More to express such duplicity in public. But Henry wanted him to do something far more reprehensible. He wanted him to swear his disloyalty in the presence of God. More understood only too clearly that for him to take an oath meant to invite God to be present as a witness and as a judge. How could he formally deny his loyalty to the very God he was calling upon to consecrate his oath? More's properly placed loyalty was built not only on a sturdy sense of self but on a great respect for his God and Church. On the other hand, Henry's fury at not being the object of misplaced loyalty was founded on pride and arrogance. His reign, as scholars have attested, was one long nightmare of "truth for ever on the scaffold, wrong for ever on the throne".[6] Despite the immense political power he wielded, Henry had little peace of mind. By contrast, More went to his death with grace and a tranquil conscience.

Loyalty for Thomas More meant that he, God, and the Catholic Church founded by Christ were much more than

[5] Ibid., p. 35.
[6] A. F. Pollard, *Henry VIII* (New York: Harper and Row, 1966), p. 351.

politicizable entities that could be tossed around and rearranged to suit anyone's pleasure. They were inviolably bound together in both reality and love and therefore demanded a loyalty that was worth more than life itself.

In the year 1535, the man who referred to himself as "the king's good servant but God's, first",[7] went to his death. On the four hundredth anniversary of that event, Pope Pius XI declared Thomas More a saint.

Commentary

Loyalty is often honored even when it is not a virtue. It is the honor that thieves have for each other and the indispensable glue that holds the Mafia together. It is the conspiracy of silence that protects professional groups from social embarrassment. It is the noble mask that hides the more ignoble motive of self-interest. It protects the guilty and sometimes assails the innocent. It is group pressure operating at the price of the dissolution of the self. As portrayed in the motion picture *The Firm,* unvirtuous loyalty is a systematic commitment to vice combined with an unrelenting disloyalty to everything that stands in its way.

Another counterfeit form of loyalty, and one that is particularly insidious inasmuch as it disguises itself as a twin virtue, is misplaced gratitude. In Shakespeare's *Henry VIII,* Cardinal Wolsey, on whose recommendation Thomas More became Speaker of the House of Commons and who preceded him as Lord Chancellor of England, expresses his undying loyalty to the king. But his loyalty is hardly

[7] Phyllis McGinley, *Saint Watching* (New York: Viking, 1969), p. III.

virtuous. Wolsey is sychophantic and unprincipled. His "loyalty" is merely a pretense to conceal his lust for gold and glory.

> ... For your great graces
> Heap'd upon me, poor undeserver, I
> Can nothing render but allegiant thanks,
> My prayers to heaven for you, my loyalty,
> Which ever has and ever shall be growing,
> Till death, that winter, kill it.[8]

Cardinal Wolsey seems to think that, because his king has been generous to him, he owes him blind loyalty. Such deformed loyalty, however, reveals his obsequiousness. On the one hand, Wolsey is too timid to challenge his king; on the other, by using vice to repay virtue, he is being false to himself. His blind loyalty is false gratitude.

Later in the play, after failing to get Rome to grant Henry a divorce, Wolsey, now charged with treason, is reduced to a pathetic figure, though he now better understands how his loyalty was misplaced: "O Cromwell, Cromwell! Had I but served my God with half the zeal I served my king, he would not in mine age have left me naked to mine enemies."[9] The words of Teresa of Avila come to mind: "Cursed be that loyalty which reaches so far as to go against the law of God."

Chesterton makes the comment that "We are all in the same boat in a stormy sea and we owe each other a terrible loyalty." In so stating, he is drawing attention to two rather

---

[8] William Shakespeare, *The Famous History of the Life of King Henry VIII*, 3.2.171–76.

[9] Ibid., 454–57. In Wolsey's own words: "If I had served God as diligently as I have done my king, He would not now have given me over to my grey hairs."

salient facts: (1) that human life is sufficiently precarious that none of us can survive alone; (2) that we need to help each other if we hope to survive. Universal loyalty, based on our common human nature, mirrors the Golden Rule of doing unto others as you would have them do unto you. It is a form of loyalty that is broad enough to exclude forms of disloyalty that result in setting factions against one another.

Henry VIII, who was not loyal to his advisors, his wives, his Church, or his God, was hardly in a moral position to command his subjects to be loyal to him. He rejected the principle of universal loyalty that would bind him to his subjects as much as his subjects would be bound to him.

King Baudouin of Belgium is the perfect antithesis of Henry VIII. Because he was loyal to all his subjects, he chose to resign his kingship rather than add his signature to an abortion bill that the Belgian Parliament had approved. Baudouin knew something about loyalties that were less than universal; he had been interned by the Nazis during World War II.

For many Belgians, their king's abdication was far more than a noble gesture. Many wrote letters to him, commending him for the political courage he showed in not abandoning his country's unborn children. His secretary, who had the task of dispatching letters of thanks to the king's supporters, was planning at that time to abort her own pregnancy. But she changed her mind and decided to give birth to her child. In reading the many glowing tributes to her king and his defense of life, she came to the conclusion that the unborn human within her must possess a dignity and value she should not violate.[10]

[10] As told to the author in a personal conversation by Professor Alice von Hildebrand, a native of Belgium, November 5, 1993, Guildford, British Columbia.

A king falls short of the responsibilities of his office when he is disloyal to any of his subjects. Henry VIII saw his kingship largely in terms of power. The context he established inevitably made a mockery of the notion of loyalty. On the other hand, Baudouin viewed the office as an opportunity to serve everyone. In this context, loyalty could mean only one thing: supporting and advancing the rights and dignity of everyone.

In his book on character building, David Isaacs writes about the virtue of loyalty in the following manner: "A loyal person accepts the bonds implicit in his relationship with others—friends, relatives, superiors, his country, its institutions, etc.—so that, as he goes on, he defends and reinforces the system of values which these represent."[11]

This statement is acceptable as long as it is kept in mind that the values that loyalty centers on are permanently linked with the universal goods of human nature. For loyalty to be virtuous, it must serve what is good. The defense of personalities, peer groups, institutions, political parties, and so on, irrespective of the values they hold, does not exemplify the virtue of loyalty. True loyalty must come to the defense of another in *reality* as well as in name.

---

[11] David Isaacs, *Character Building: A Guide for Parents and Teachers* (County Dublin, Ire.: Four Courts Press, 1984), p. 133.

MEEKNESS

IN GERMANY, during the Nazi era, there was a Dominican preacher who was renowned for his fervor and courage. He spoke fearlessly and relentlessly against Nazi ideology. The Gestapo had been reluctant to arrest him because it did not want to provoke the large circle of followers who had great admiration and affection for him. When he was finally arrested and hung, the friars of his Order begged for the release of his body. The body was returned, grudgingly. It bore the unmistakable marks of brutal torture. Orders were posted that the priest's funeral be a private affair and warned that anyone who attended would be interrogated.

Karl Schmidt, also a strong voice against Hitler and the Nazi regime, had been a close friend of the friar. He dared to attend the funeral. As a result, he was arrested the next morning and conscripted into the German army as a foot soldier. He was told that if he refused to go to the Russian front, his entire family would be sent to a concentration camp.

Schmidt was soon captured by the Soviet Army and sent to a slave labor camp, where he remained for seven seemingly interminable years. When the war ended he was "invited" to become a Communist and reside in Russia. He was told that his family no longer cared about him, the alleged proof being that no one ever wrote to him despite the fact that he wrote letters to them every week. When he refused, his time of imprisonment was extended. But Schmidt never lost faith. He said the Rosary daily and taught his fellow inmates to pray and not yield to the temptation of despair.

Schmidt was finally released in a prisoner-exchange arrangement. By virtue of an association of ex-prisoners that he later formed, he discovered that the letter-writing scheme had been a cruel hoax. None of the families ever received any of the letters that were sent from the Gulag. It was all a calculated attempt to brainwash the prisoners into believing that their loved ones had given up on them. But there was an extraordinary exception. Four times a year Schmidt's letters reached their intended destinations. Each time the letter's postmark bore the date of a major feast day of Mary, the Mother of God.

Schmidt made it back to his hometown in Germany. He was initially overjoyed to see Canadian soldiers everywhere and to learn that the German army was retreating toward Berlin. When he arrived at his house he found his mother in tears amid family belongings that were lying in ruins. It was not the Gestapo that had ransacked the house, however, it was Canadian soldiers who had assumed, not entirely without reason, that the Schmidts were Nazis. One of the more attractive items the soldiers pilferred was a camera that was Schmidt's prized possession. This was by no means an ordinary camera. It was an experimental model that had two apertures and several lenses that simultaneously exposed photographic paper to light coming in from different angles. When the film was developed, the photographs could be placed in a special viewer to reveal a strikingly three-dimensional image. This highly specialized camera was relatively unknown, and only a few models of its kind were ever produced. Because the soldier who stole it was not familiar with its peculiarities, he understandably neglected to take the viewer.

Several years later, one of Karl Schmidt's two sons, Josef, now a Catholic priest, was visiting with a priest friend of his. They were engaged in a conversation with a third member of the cloth, a well-known theologian who taught at a distinguished Canadian university. This theologian, upon learning of Josef's German ancestry, offered to show him a "marvelous invention" he had picked up when he was in Germany after the war. Father Josef inspected the invention with astonishment mingled with a sense of horror. "Where did you get it?" Father Josef asked. The theologian replied, "Oh ... during the war I was with the Canadian army when we went to Germany. I stayed with a family there. We got to be fairly close. They gave this to me when I left."[1] He mentioned the town; it was the same town in Germany where the Schmidts lived.

Father Josef turned the camera over and over in his hands. He read the initials engraved on its tiny brass plate: K. S. There could be little doubt. The theologian had stolen the camera from the Karl Schmidt household. What should be done? It is easy enough to imagine the anger that might have been rising in Josef's heart. Should he confront and expose the theologian? This would certainly prove embarrassing, even humiliating, possibly damaging to his illustrious reputation. Yet hypocrisy and thievery should be dealt with swiftly and decisively. What would his father do; what would Christ have done in such a situation? It took

[1] Michael O'Brien, "The Gift", *Nazareth Journal,* Advent 1991, pp. 13–16. The story is true, though the names of individuals mentioned have been changed to preserve their privacy.

an extraordinary act of meekness on Josef's part not to avenge his father right then and there.

Father Josef wrote to his father, informing him of his surprising discovery. He also spoke to his sister about this amazing coincidence, or "God-incident", as he preferred to call it.

A few months later, on Christmas eve, Father Josef once again encountered the theologian. But there was no confrontation or exposure. He handed him a curious item that caused the theologian's hands to tremble and his face to turn crimson. "It's for you", he said gently. "The man who gave you the camera says to you, God bless you. He says that he forgot to give you the viewer that goes with it." It was a gesture worthy of the good bishop that Victor Hugo portrayed in *Les Misérables.* If Karl Schmidt had learned anything from his many years of suffering and privation, it was that it is better to counter vice with virtue than to answer vice with an avenging vice of one's own. Whatever inclination he might have felt toward anger, revenge, retaliation, or strict justice was/overcome by the power of his meekness so that he could express, in their stead, humility, forgiveness, generosity, and charity. It was because of his meekness that his "better angels" could prevail and announce their Christmas message of peace and love to all men of good will.

Commentary

To the list of popular slogans that belittle virtue, which includes "chaste makes waste" and "humility is senility", we could add "meekness is weakness." It is a pity that meekness is among the least-appreciated virtues, because "meekness above all", noted Thomas Aquinas, "makes a man self-possessed."[2]

Meekness is actually the opposite of weakness; it is power. Indeed, Aquinas' term for self-possession, *"compos sui"*, expresses the idea of "empowerment". *Compos* (accusative: *compotem*) literally means "having mastery" or "having power", the interior power by which one can come into possession of himself. According to Samuel Johnson's *Dictionary,* the word "nincompoop" is derived from *non compos* or not having mastery over oneself.

People speak approvingly of someone "going ballistic" in the face of even a slight offense. "Feminist rage" is presumed justified on the basis of the acceptability of revenge for perceived injustices. But the unleashing of wrath is not the empowerment that Aquinas had in mind. The anger that leads to revenge can be futile, if not counterproductive. As Saint Bonaventure warned, becoming upset and impatient over the failings of someone is like responding to his falling into a ditch by throwing oneself into another. If the desire for vengeance is not restrained, the administration of justice becomes merely a repayment of evil with another evil. And retaliation of this kind has a tendency to escalate conflict, with each blow being repaid with yet another.

Empowerment needs meekness to be effective as well as virtuous. Meekness enables a person to do good in response to evil. Meekness is not cowardliness, timidity, or servility; it is the power that restrains the onslaught of anger and subjects it to the order of reason. Theophylact, the eleventh century archbishop of Achris, said the meek "are not

---

[2] Thomas Aquinas, *Summa Theologiae,* II–II, 157, 4: "Mansuetudo maxime facit hominem esse compotem sui."

those who are never at all angry, for such are insensible: but those who, feeling anger, control it, and are angry only when they ought to be. Meekness excludes revenge, irritability, morbid sensitivity, but not self-defense, or a quiet and steady maintenance of right." Meekness is the inner strength that allows a person to bear evils or difficulties without whining or cringing. It conquers dissipating passions so that prudence and love can do their more important work. As Mother Teresa of Calcutta has said, it is better to do good than fight evil.

Saint Bernard pointed out several centuries ago that there were individuals who appear to be very meek as long as everything goes their way, but as soon as they encounter some contradiction or adversity, they flare up and begin to smoke like volcanoes. They may be said to be burning coals hidden under ashes; they are meek only to a point.

One of the greatest examples of meekness to a heroic degree is that of Maximilian Kolbe. While a prisoner at Auschwitz, Kolbe, a Franciscan priest, showed love for his captors no matter how brutally they treated him. He implored his fellow inmates to resist the temptation to hate the Nazis, telling them that only love is creative.

When ten men were selected to die in reprisal for a prisoner's escape, Kolbe volunteered to take the place of one who pleaded for mercy. "I am a Catholic priest", Kolbe said to the *Lagerführer.* "I want to die for that man; I am old; he has a wife and children."[3] During their final agonizing days in a starvation bunker, Kolbe exhorted the nine men dying with him to pray for their enemies as well as for themselves.

[3] Diana Dewar, *The Saint of Auschwitz: The Story of Maximilian Kolbe* (San Francisco: Harper and Row, 1982), p. 110.

Kolbe's meekness, no doubt, had supernatural origins. In the face of some of the greatest evil known to man, he never relinquished the conviction that good would ultimately triumph. He believed that although pain and persecution can destroy a man's body, when accepted in love for others, they can perfect a man's soul. In June 1979, when Pope John Paul II visited Auschwitz, he said, "A victory through faith and love was won by him [Kolbe] in this place, which was built for the negation of faith."[4] Three years later, on the eight hundredth anniversary of Saint Francis of Assisi's birth, he declared Kolbe a saint.

[4] Ibid., p. ix.

MERCY

WHILE VISITING the prison in Potsdam, Germany, King Frederick William I (1688–1740) listened to a number of pleas for pardon from prisoners who claimed to be victims of injustice. All swore they had suffered imprisonment on account of prejudiced judges, perjured witnesses, and unscrupulous lawyers. From cell to cell, allegations of wronged innocence and false imprisonment continued until the king came to the door of a cell occupied by a surly inmate who said nothing. Surprised at his silence, Frederick remarked, somewhat sarcastically, "Well I suppose you are innocent too." "No, your Majesty", came the startling response. "I am guilty and richly deserve all that I get." "Here, turnkey", thundered Frederick, "come and get rid of this rascal quick, before he corrupts this fine lot of innocent people that you are responsible for."[1]

The wise king offered mercy and pardon to this prisoner because he was willing to accept his just penalty. We find a parallel to King Frederick William I's expression of mercy in Heinrich von Kleist's play *Prince Frederick of Homburg,* where the character representing the king's grandfather— Frederick William (1620–1688)—also dispenses mercy and pardon. In both these stories—the historical and the fictional—mercy is ministered only after justice is accepted.

[1] Edward Fuller (ed.), *Thesaurus of Anecdotes* (New York: Crown Publishers, 1942), p. 50.

The play opens with Frederick William, the Elector of Brandenburg, making plans for the Battle of Fehrbellin against the Swedes (1675). Prince Frederick of Homburg, the elector's son, is in charge of the cavalry and under strict orders to await the signal from his father before he attacks and delivers the finishing blow. The prince, however, has been dreaming of accomplishing heroic feats and winning Princess Nathalie's love. Because of his dreams and his strong desire for personal glory, he does not heed the elector's orders and leads his troops into battle.

Despite his victory, the prince has disobeyed the elector's orders. He is subsequently tried and condemned to die by a court martial. The prince becomes panic-stricken and abjectly begs first his mother and then Nathalie to intercede on his behalf to save his life. He is willing to be demoted, discharged, or even dishonored; anything but be put to death. Although they are disappointed by his display of cowardice, they nevertheless plead with the elector to pardon him. Moved by Nathalie's sincere entreaties and desirous to spare the life of his own son, the elector allows the prince to decide for himself whether the death sentence was just: "If you maintain you've suffered an injustice, I beg of you to send me word at once, and I will send your sabre back to you."[2] But the prince refuses to send such word, preferring to give the matter more thought. After considerable soul-searching, the prince's nobler self emerges. He concludes that his father has dealt with him justly: "If I must argue with him for my pardon, I'd just as soon know nothing of his mercy."[3] He then, in effect, signs his own

[2] Heinrich von Kleist, *Prince Frederick of Homburg,* trans. Peggy Sherry, in *Plays,* ed. Walter Hinderer (New York: Continuum, 1982), p. 321.

[3] Ibid., p. 324.

death sentence. Subsequently, in the presence of the electorate, he formally concedes the validity of his sentence. He then proudly asserts the code of honor and patriotic service and fully acknowledges that a commander must first of all learn to obey.

> ... now that I have thought it over,
> I wish to die the death decreed for me!
> ... It is my absolute desire
> To glorify the sacred code of battle,
> Broken by me before the entire army,
> With voluntary death.[4]

Now that the prince is willing to accept justice, he is eligible for mercy. When the elector hears these courageous words, he is overjoyed. He tears up the death sentence, pardons the prince, and grants him permission to marry Nathalie. The prince is thereby restored to life, honor, and happiness. On this joyful note, the play ends.

Commentary

The Latin word for mercy is *misericordia,* which itself is composed of the words: *miserum,* which means "sorrow" (or "misery"), and *cordia,* which refers to the "heart"; in combination, these two words signify that which flows from one who is "sorrowful at heart". The etymology of the word does not offer a complete definition of mercy, but it does point us in the right direction.

Mercy is more than compassion, which is also a heartfelt sorrow at another's misfortunes. Whereas compassion does

[4] Ibid., p. 336.

empathize with the sufferer, it does not do more than that. Mercy, however, removes suffering.

A merciful person (*misericors*) is sorrowful at heart (*miserum cor*) over another person's misery as if it were his own. It follows then, that such a person would endeavor to dispel that misery, which is the effect of mercy. At the same time, mercy is not to be equated with generosity. The latter virtue is not necessarily a response to another's misery. Generosity may be directed toward a happy person. Nor does generosity have to be concerned about justice. But mercy is exquisitely poised between the demands of justice and the disposition of the sufferer. "It does not destroy justice", as Thomas Aquinas notes, "but is a certain kind of fulfillment of justice."[5] "Mercy without justice is the mother of dissolution", he writes; but also, "justice without mercy is cruelty."[6]

Mercy is truly a gift; it is a gift aimed at relieving the sorrowful of their sorrow and offered in such a way that it does not collide with justice. Given this profile of mercy, it is not hard to understand why the ancients associated mercy with the Divinity:

> Mercy the wise Athenians held to be
> Not an affection, but a Deity.[7]

"Wilt thou draw near the nature of the gods? Draw near them in being merciful", wrote Shakespeare, "sweet mercy is nobility's true badge."[8] The wisdom, liberality, and

[5] Thomas Aquinas, *Summa Theologiae*, I, 21, 4 ad 2: "Misericordia non tollit iustitiam, sed est quaedam iustitia plenitudo."

[6] Joseph Pieper, *The Four Cardinal Virtues* (New York: Harcourt, Brace and World, 1965), p. 112.

[7] Robert Herrick, "Mercy".

[8] William Shakespeare, *Titus Andronicus*, 1.1.118.

readiness to forgive that mercy presupposes give mercy a godlike quality. The unexpected suddenness by which it is dispensed also makes one mindful of the Deity. In thinking about a man who fell into a river and drowned, Saint Augustine commented in his *Confessions* that "the mercy of God may be found between the bridge and the stream."

Being merciful is not so lofty that it is out of human reach. It does not cost us much to be merciful, and we do not have to front grave dangers in the process. Laurence Sterne, one of the most original writers in English literature, proclaimed, "We must imitate the Deity in all his moral attributes, but mercy is the only one in which we can pretend to equal him. . . . We cannot, indeed, give like God, but surely we may forgive like him."

The secular world commonly lionizes justice and speaks glowingly of the prospect of a "just society" but is strangely taciturn when it comes to mercy. "To err is human, to forgive is against departmental policy", reads a sign in a Los Angeles police station. And since mercy is available only to the contrite, we should not forget that, while "to err is human, to admit it is superhuman." One must swallow his pride before he can drink from the chalice of mercy.

The poet Shelley is gravely mistaken when he states that the distinction between mercy and justice was invented in the courts of tyrants. "Mercy seasons justice",[9] as Shakespeare rightly says; but it is not a meal in itself. It needs justice as salt needs the meat it flavors. To pardon the unrepentent is not to offer mercy but to negate justice. Mercy follows justice and perfects it; but it does not replace it. Its essence is not license. Mercy can flourish only when it

[9] William Shakespeare, *The Merchant of Venice*, 4.1.197.

is in a context of justice. Accordingly, C. S. Lewis has stated that "Mercy will flower only when it grows in the crannies of the rock of Justice: transplanted to the marshlands of mere Humanitarianism, it becomes a man-eating weed, all the more dangerous because it is still called by the same name as the mountain variety."[10]

Mercy is humane not only because it crowns justice but, more importantly, because it acknowledges the infirmities of human nature. It is not unjust to hold a person to a standard of justice. But it may be inhuman to withhold mercy when a person fails to meet that standard. We should be prepared to extend mercy to others in the measure we hope to receive it ourselves. To be merciless to others is to suppress the truth of our own fallibility.

> Being all fashioned of the self-same dust,
> Let us be merciful as well as just.[11]

Justice is rational and measured; mercy is immeasurable. Justice can be commanded; mercy must be freely given. There are halls for justice, but there are hearts for mercy. Magistrates are just; the godly are merciful. Justice is embodied in the law; mercy transcends the law. The law must be studied; mercy must be practiced.

> Reason to rule, but mercy to forgive:
> The first is law, the last prerogative.[12]

Mercy lacks the heroic quality associated with virtues

[10] C. S. Lewis, "Punishment and Responsibility", *Morality in Practice,* ed. James P. Sterba (Belmont, Calif.: Wadsworth Publishing, 1984), p. 266.

[11] Henry Wadsworth Longfellow, *Tales of a Wayside Inn,* 3.

[12] John Dryden, *The Hind and the Panther,* 1.

such as courage and determination. It does not possess the primacy enjoyed by reverence and humility. Nor does it have the independent character of generosity and integrity. It is a complementary virtue, one that is destined to share the spotlight with a more fundamental good. The nineteenth-century American clergyman Edwin Hubbell Chapin expressed it most eloquently when he wrote: "Mercy among the virtues is like the moon among the stars,—not so sparkling and vivid as many, but dispensing a calm radiance that hallows the whole. It is the bow that rests upon the bosom of the cloud when the storm is past. It is the light that hovers above the judgment-seat."

MIRTHFULNESS

GOOD COMMUNICATORS are made, not born. A good illustration of this axiom is Norman Cousins, who, by dint of uncommon hard work applied to common sense, became one of the outstanding communicators of our time. The first time he lectured at New York City's Town Hall, then a mecca for public speakers, he was considerably less than scintillating. After his presentation, Bennett Cerf, the book publisher and avid collector of jokes, came up to him and advised that he season his talks with a bit of humor. "Start with a humorous story", he advised. "It's always a good idea to involve yourself in the anecdote, especially if a celebrity or two figures in the story. Hasn't anything funny happened to you recently that also involves someone who's famous?" Cousins recalled a recent occasion in which his pretalk jitters were sufficiently apparent to prompt the solicitude of the person sitting next to him, who happened to be Dwight David Eisenhower. "What's the matter? You look a little pale", the General inquired. Cousins whispered back that the prospect of speaking to an assemblage of distinguished educators robed in university gowns was rather intimidating. "Do as I do", said Eisenhower, "Whenever I feel nervous before I speak I use a little trick.... I look out at the people in the audience and just imagine that everyone out there is sitting in his tattered old underwear."[1]

[1] Norman Cousins, *Head First: The Biology of Hope* (New York: E. P. Dutton, 1989), p. 129.

Bennett Cerf was delighted by Cousins' story and strongly urged him to use it in his next public presentation. Two weeks later, Cousins spoke in St. Louis and began by relating the Eisenhower incident. It failed to produce even a ripple. The audience was grim and stony-faced. The rest of the talk was a painful and humorless uphill battle.

Following the lecture, a man came up to him and questioned whether the anecdote Cousins told about Eisenhower were true. Cousins, naturally, insisted that it was. "That's strange", said the man; "Bennett Cerf lectured here last week and said it happened to him."[2]

Cousins did not allow this innocent embarrassment to discourage him from using humorous anecdotes in future talks. In fact, he used them well and with great success. Cerf had given him good advice, if not good example. Cousins became not only a confident and successful speaker but a keen student of humor. He was editor of the *Saturday Review* for more than twenty-five years. During his tenure, he was fond of concocting off-the-wall, humorous notices for the magazine's "Personals" section. A few examples of his light-hearted mischief:[3]

WE WISH TO APOLOGIZE publicly to 796 members of the World Stamp Collectors' Society who went to Norwalk, Connecticut, instead of Norwalk, California, for our annual convention because of printer's error on invitation.
M. G. Stuckey, President
WSCS. SR Box AC.

DISTRESS SALE: Marginally defective calculators (pocket size). Guaranteed to be 98% accurate. Perfect gift for easy-going students, tax accountants, stockbrokers.
WM, Box R.R.

[2] Ibid., p. 130.
[3] Ibid., 147–50.

NOTICE to our Denture Stick-Tite customers: Our scientists have devised a workable release solvent. Consequently, our thanks to wearers who were stuck with old formula.
SR/W Box N.S.

INSOMNIA A PROBLEM? Fall asleep instantly by listening to our LP readings of congressional rollcall votes.
Write: Surplus Sound Co.
SR/W Box W.G.

Surmising that mirth could contribute to good health, Cousins spent years researching the subject. His book *Head First: The Biology of Hope* provides an impressive inventory of evidence that mirth can help combat disease, even that which is serious.

For example, laughter can release endorphins, which act as the body's own naturally produced pain-reducing agents. It also can contribute to improved functioning of the immune system. And it provides an invaluable form of exercise for a number of internal organs, a kind of "internal jogging", as Cousins likes to call it.

Cousins' book also demonstrates that laughter reduces "discomfort sensitivity" and improves a patient's outlook on life and suffering. Researchers Rod Martin and Herbert Lefcourt of the University of Waterloo have discovered a positive correlation between an appreciation of humor and an ability to cope with personal problems and life's stresses.

Cousins is in good company when he argues that mirth contributes to health and well-being. After all, Scripture tells us that "A cheerful heart is good medicine."[4] "Frame your mind to mirth and merriment," notes Shakespeare,

[4] Prov 17:22.

"which bars a thousand harms and lengthens life."[5] "Laughter, the Best Medicine" has been a *Reader's Digest* regular feature for many years.

There are growing numbers of physicians, nurses, psychologists, and patients who use mirth to reduce stress, ease pain, foster recovery, and generally brighten one's outlook on life. For this, Norman Cousins, perhaps more than any other person, deserves no small amount of credit.

Commentary

A nineteenth-century Nova Scotian humorist by the name of Thomas C. Haliburton has spoken wittily, wisely, and well about the virtues of mirth:

> There is nothing like fun, is there? I haven't had any myself, but I do like it in others. We need all the counterweights we can muster to balance the sad relations in life. God has made sunny spots in the heart; why should we exclude the light from them?

These "sunny spots" make it clear enough that mirthfulness is a divinely instituted virtue and a practical indication of God's mercy. If worry is a weight, then mirth is its counterweight; the one being gravity, the other being levity.

> Care to our coffin adds a nail, no doubt
> And every grin, so merry, draws one out.[6]

And, to modify Shakespeare, the winter of our discontent is made glorious summer by laughter. Or, as Victor Hugo remarks: "Laughter is the sun that drives winter from the human face."

Among the philosophers who are identified with mirth

---

[5] William Shakespeare, *The Taming of the Shrew,* introduction, 2.137.

[6] John Wolcot, English satiric poet (1738–1819).

is Democritus, a Greek cosmologist who was born around 460 B.C., whose emphasis on the value of good humor in his ethical teaching earned him the title of the "laughing philosopher". Among the saints who are identified with mirth is Sir Thomas More. Erasmus said of him, "From boyhood he was always so pleased with a joke that it might seem that jesting was the main object of his life."[7] In adulthood, "His countenance answers to his character, having an expression of kind and friendly cheerfulness with a little air of raillery."[8]

More's death sentence, by a perverse and petulant king, did nothing to dampen his gaiety. During his last days, while in prison and suffering from his old disease of the chest—gravel, stone, and the cramp—he habitually joked with his family and friends, whenever they were permitted to see him, as merrily as in the old days at Chelsea. When it came time for him to ascend the executioner's scaffold, it was discovered that its structure was so weak that it appeared ready to collapse. Turning to the man assisting him, More remarked, "I pray you, I pray you, Mr. Lieutenant, see me safe up, and for my coming down let me shift for myself." After kneeling and saying prayers, he then turned to the executioner and, with a cheerful countenance, spoke to him: "Pluck up thy spirits, man, and be not afraid to do thine office. My neck is very short. Take heed therefore thou strike not awry for saving thine honor."[9]

Humor depends on a person's ability to detect the incongruous. Laughter is a healthy and health-giving way of

[7] Erasmus, "Letter of Erasmus to Ulrich von Hutten", in Thomas More, *Utopia* (Princeton, N.J.: Van Nostrand, 1947), p. 192.

[8] Ibid., p. 189.

[9] William Roper, *The Life of Sir Thomas More* in More, *Utopia,* pp. 279–80.

dealing with opposite lines of logic that suddenly collide with each other:

> Dieting is a victory of mind over platter.
> He who agitates is tossed.
> A rolling stone gathers no boss.
> Love is a comedy of Eros.
> It is better to have loved a short girl
> than never to have loved a tall.

Children are nature's best laughers, perhaps because they are too young to take anything too seriously. Dostoevsky remarks in his novel *The Adolescent*, "Children are the only human creatures to produce perfect laughter and that's just what makes them so enchanting. I find a crying child repulsive whereas a laughing child is a sunbeam from paradise for me, a revelation of future bliss when man will finally become as pure and simple-hearted as a babe."

Fountains of humor exist almost everywhere. People need only the wit to see them. What's in a name? Quite possibly gales of laughter, if the name is sufficiently odd. The Society for the Verification and Enjoyment of Fascinating Names of Actual Persons (SVEFNAP) has authenticated the following as bona fide names of actual human beings: Miss Addylou Ebfisty Plunt, Onofly Steffuk, Wiggo Norwang, A. Smerling Lecher, Fice Mork, M. Tugrul Uke, Burke Uzzle, Sexious Boonjug, Polly Wanda Crocker, Dulcie Pillage, P. V. Glob, Clela Rorex, Zilpher Spittle, Dunwoody Zook, and Sir Ranulph Twisleton-Wykeham-Fiennes.

Correcting exams may not be so tedious if one's students have mastered the mirthful art of fracturing famous figures. Consider the following dozen compound fractures culled from from a collection compiled by history teacher Richard Lederer.

Socrates died from an overdose of wedlock.

Homer wrote the "Oddity" in which Penelope was the last hardship that Ulysses endured on his journey.

David fought with the Philatelists.

Solomon, one of David's sons, had 500 wives and 500 porcupines.

King Arthur lived in the Age of Shivery.

Martin Luther died a horrible death, being excommunicated by a bull.

Donatello's interest in the female form made him the father of the Renaissance.

Shakespeare was famous only because of his plays.

Voltaire invented electricity and wrote a book called *Candy*.

Thomas Jefferson, a virgin, and Benjamin Franklin were two singers of the Declaration of Independence.

Lincoln's mother died in infancy, and he was born in a log cabin which he built with his own hands.

Most humor is inadvertent; it often is the result of an embarrassing mistake. Therefore we need humility, as well as wit, to have a sense of humor. G. K. Chesterton warned people against taking themselves too seriously. "Seriousness is not a virtue", he wrote, and he reminded us that levity, as well as levitation, are characteristics of great saints. According to Chesterton, "Satan fell by the force of gravity", whereas "Angels can fly because they can take themselves lightly."[10] We should be humble enough to retain our lightness and our humor even when the joke is on us.

[10] G. K. Chesterton, *Orthodoxy* (Garden City, N.Y.: Doubleday, 1959), pp. 120–21.

MODESTY

FLANNERY O'CONNOR is acknowledged as one of the most original and provocative writers of our time. She has been ranked with Mark Twain and F. Scott Fitzgerald among America's finest prose stylists. Given her literary accomplishments, it was once suggested to her that someone would write her biography. O'Connor dismissed the notion. "There won't be any biographies of me", she said, "for only one reason, lives spent between the house and the chicken yard do not make exciting copy."[1]

She was alluding to the illness that confined her to her mother's chicken farm in Milledgeville, Georgia, a few miles outside of Atlanta. Lupus erythematosus, a devastating and incurable neurological disorder that can be kept at bay only with drugs and a highly disciplined existence, had claimed her father. It ended O'Connor's life when she was thirty-nine. She gave herself daily injections, hobbled around on aluminum crutches, and could write for no more than two hours a day. What she was able to accomplish, given her infirmity, was remarkable. But she did not complain. In fact, she regarded sickness before death a very appropriate occurrence that allowed her to receive special mercies from

---

[1] Paul Gray, "Letters of Flannery O'Connor", *Time*, March 5, 1979, p. 69.

God. "To expect too much", she held, "is to have a senti-mental view of life."[2]

She was wrong about the literary world's interest in her. Her letters, published under the title *A Habit of Being,* brought her added fame after she died. The collection made the best-seller list and established Flannery O'Connor as the most memorable character she ever transcribed to paper.[3]

Throughout the 617 pages of correspondence, she either ignored her deteriorating health or mentioned it offhandedly. In one letter she wrote: "I owe my existence to the pitui-tary glands of thousands of pigs butchered daily in Chicago, Illinois, at the Armour packing plant. If pigs wore garments, I wouldn't be worthy to kiss the hems of them." She saw even her use of crutches as an occasion to laugh at herself: "My greatest exertion and pleasure these last years has been throwing the garbage to the chickens and I can still do this, though I am in danger of going with it."[4]

She abhorred pomposity of any stripe and sprinkled her letters with plenty of "ain'ts" and "naws". She also expressed wariness of "innerleckchuls".[5] To a correspondent who had expressed uneasiness in writing to a celebrity, she pointed out that fame is "a comic distinction shared with Roy Rogers' horse and Miss Watermelon of 1955". Her letter-writing was unimpeachably democratic. "Mail is very eventful to me", she said, "I never mind writing anybody."[6]

[2] Cecelia McGowan, "The Faith of Flannery O'Connor", *The Catholic Digest,* February 1983, p. 78.

[3] Flannery O'Connor, *The Habit of Being,* ed. Sally Fitzgerald (Farrar, Straus and Giroux, 1979).

[4] Gray, loc. cit. p. 69.

[5] Marion Montgomery, *The Trouble with You Innerleckchuls* (Front Royal, Vir.: Christendom, 1988), p. 10.

[6] Gray, loc. cit. p. 68.

Étienne Gilson said that Thomas Aquinas possessed two virtues to an exceptional degree: a perfect intellectual modesty and an almost reckless intellectual audacity.[7] Much the same could be said of O'Connor. There was not the slightest hint of sentimentality in her view of life. Her intellectual modesty allowed her to see things as they really are, and her intellectual audacity gave her the nerve to be painfully candid. "If you live today you breathe in nihilism", she said. "In or out of the Church, it's the gas you breathe."[8]

O'Connor audaciously tackled the nihilistic assumptions of modern philosophy with stories about ordinary people from her own backyard. The culture of O'Connor's South was shaped, in part, by class-conscious social behavior, sentimentalized reminiscences of the antebellum golden age, and rationalizations of the injustices that remained from the legacy of slavery. Understanding the smugness of the Southern middle class, O'Connor saw, perhaps more plainly than most, the self-satisfaction that was spreading throughout the country during the postwar prosperity of the 1950s. Her characters, like herself, inhabit a narrow world, but their relevance reaches far beyond it.

O'Connor used her art to shake and sharpen the sensibilities of an American society that had grown morally soft and philosophically unfocused. She created shocking characters and narrated their misdeeds with graphic grotesqueness in order to jolt people back to an awareness of reality. The unvarnished truth her stories expose is that we are all grotesque, in some way or another. But there is hope, even for the grotesque.

O'Connor's realism was informed by her Catholic faith.

[7] Étienne Gilson, *Reason and Revelation in the Middle Ages* (New York: Charles Scribner's Sons, 1938), p. 71.

[8] O'Connor, loc. cit. p. 97.

"For I am no disbeliever in spiritual purpose and no vague believer. I see from the standpoint of Christian orthodoxy. This means for me the meaning of life is centered in our Redemption in Christ and what I see in the world I see in relation to that. I don't think that this is a position that can be taken halfway or one that is particularly easy in these times to make transparent in fiction."[9] Her modesty allowed her to realize the difficulty of her task, and it protected her from discouragement when her art was misunderstood by both critics and the general public. Unintimidated by popular trends or prominent people, she remained faithful to her vision to the end.

Commentary

The modest person does not draw undue attention to himself. He is self-assured, but not self-absorbed. He is temperate in dress, language, and comportment and has a strong sense of the value of his privacy. He knows that being a person is fundamentally incompatible with being an object for public consumption. Modesty is, as it were, his body's conscience. He is not interested in displaying his talents and attainments for people to admire. He even shuns making himself the subject of conversation. He is more eager to know what he needs to know than to parade what he already knows. He has a healthy sense of himself as he is and is less concerned about how others view him. His enthusiasms center around what is real. Therefore he has little patience

[9] Bruce Edwards, "Flannery O'Connor and the Literary Temple", *New Oxford Review*, April 1984, p. 18.

with flattery and adulation. Nor is he inclined to exaggerate or boast. The modest person is aware of his limitations and retains the capacity to blush.

Modesty is a virtue that is difficult to describe since, by nature, it tends to withdraw from view. It operates somewhat like a catalyst that does not do anything itself but assists other things in working more efficiently. In this regard it is like a perfume that loses its fragrance once it is exposed. Diogenes called modesty "the color of virtue" because it heightens other virtues the way shading makes colors in a painting appear more vivid and realistic. Modesty makes a beautiful person appear to be even more beautiful.

Mark Twain averred that "Man is the only animal that blushes. Or needs to." A person blushes when he is suddenly the object of praise or attention. It catches him off guard at a moment when he is interested in something other than himself. The essence of modesty is self-forgetfulness.

Abraham Lincoln's "Gettysburg Address" and the events immediately connected with it comprise a noteworthy illustration of the virtue of modesty. Although he was not the main speaker for the occasion, Lincoln produced five slightly different versions of his speech, all of which he wrote out by hand. What was uppermost in his mind was the solemnity of the occasion, which was the dedication of the Gettysburg battlefield as a cemetery for those who had lost their lives in the great Civil War battle that was fought there. It was most fitting, therefore, for him to say that "The world will little note, nor long remember what we say here, but it can never forget what they did here." Lincoln's self-effacement, entirely appropriate for the occasion, helped to make his words far more memorable than he could have imagined at the time. The text of his speech at Gettysburg is carved on a stone plaque at the Lincoln Memorial in the nation's capital. What is sewn in self-forgetfulness is more likely to endure than what is produced with applause in mind.

Edward Everett was the principal speaker on that same day, November 19, 1863. Moved by the gracefulness of the President's words and the nobility of his tone, he wrote to Lincoln and humbly confessed that "I should be glad if I could flatter myself that I came as near to the central idea of the occasion in two hours as you did in two minutes."[10] Lincoln answered Everett's letter the same day he received it, November 20, 1863. He stated that under the circumstances Everett could not have been excused to make a short address, nor he himself a long one. "I am pleased to know that, in your judgment," Lincoln went on to write, "the little I did say was not entirely a failure."[11]

Modesty is a most attractive virtue, though it disappears as soon as it is used specifically for that purpose. Modesty forbids self-advertisement or private calculation. Dame Edith Sitwell once said that she often wished she had time to cultivate modesty, but was too busy thinking about herself.[12] Although her remark was said in jest, it does illustrate a truism, namely, that self-centeredness can prevent modesty from taking root.

Whereas modesty enhances other virtues, immodesty calls so much attention to itself that hardly anything else can be noticed. Immodesty, therefore, can conceal personality. The popular maxim, "If you've got it, flaunt it", fails

[10] *The Collected Works of Abraham Lincoln,* ed. Roy P. Basler (New Brunswick, N.J.: Rutgers University Press, 1953), p. 25.

[11] Ibid., p. 24.

[12] Edith Sitwell, *Observer,* April 30, 1950.

to take into account the more important dimension of a person's inner life. Modesty allows the beauty of one's personality to shine forth without the disturbing element of pride.

Immodesty is more conspicuous than modesty, but essentially because of its superficiality. It does not require much depth of perception to notice a display of flamboyance. Hollywood, the world's capital of glamor, glitter, and glitz, enables people to make an entire career out of being immodest. All this is only too well known. In a materialistic world, the subtleties of modesty are easily overlooked.

If immodesty parades superficiality, modesty safeguards a mystery. The poet Richard Crashaw suggests metaphorically that modest self-effacement allows us to recognize the presence of God. In referring to the miracle at Cana in which Christ changed water into wine, he states: "The unconscious waters saw their God and blushed."[13]

[13] Cited in Fulton J. Sheen, *Life of Christ* (New York: McGraw-Hill, 1958), p. 77.

PATIENCE

A FTER SUFFERING the double tragedy of his father's suicide and his mother's death the following year in an auto accident, Walker Percy was adopted at the age of fourteen by his uncle. Uncle Will, a prominent Mississippi lawyer, published poet, and friend of Carl Sandburg, William Faulkner, and the psychiatrist Harry Stack Sullivan, introduced his nephew to Brahms, Shakespeare, and Keats. Yet Percy's formal education up to the age of thirty was almost entirely scientific. He certainly did not have any plans to be a writer.

Percy received his medical degree with high honors from Columbia University. While interning at New York's Bellevue Hospital, he performed many autopsies on indigent alcoholics, many of whom had died of tuberculosis. He contracted the highly contagious disease and was sent to a sanatorium in upstate New York for a long period of rest. After more than two years of convalescence, he assumed the post of instructor in pathology at Columbia medical school. But within a few months he suffered a relapse and was sent to a home in Connecticut, where, it is said, he occupied the same bed formerly used by four-time Pulitzer Prize winning playwright Eugene O'Neill. He needed another year of treatment and convalescence.

The young medical doctor, who had been, by his own admission, obsessed with rigorous scientific inquiry, had himself become an object of constant scrutiny and evaluation. The man who had planned to spend his career helping others was almost completely cut off from the outside world. But he was not inactive; he used this enforced passivity as an active instrument. He read and he thought. He contemplated the healing potential of the word as a "symbol". If medicine can heal, may not words also be put to a healing purpose? He read copiously and began writing philosophical articles. "I was in bed so much, alone so much, that I had nothing to do but read and think", he said. "Then I gradually began to realize that as a scientist—a doctor, pathologist—I knew a great deal *about* man but had little idea of what man *is*."[1]

What began to interest him was no longer the physiological and pathological processes that went on in the human body but the problem of man himself, his nature and destiny; specifically and more immediately, the predicament of man in a modern technological society. "If the first great intellectual discovery of my life was the beauty of the scientific method," he wrote, "surely the second was the discovery of the singular predicament of man in the very world which has been transformed by science."

He read Aquinas, Heidegger, Tolstoy, Kierkegaard, and Camus. He learned from Dostoevsky how hungry we are for faith and how hard it is to find and keep. He learned from Simone Weil's *Waiting on God* (a phrase she borrowed from Pascal) the need to be a patient pilgrim.[2] From

---

[1] Robert Coles, "Profiles (Walker Percy—Part I)", *New Yorker,* October 2, 1978, p. 50.

[2] Simone Weil, *Waiting on God,* trans. Emma Craufurd (Glasgow, Scot.: William Collins, 1950). In giving this work its title, the publisher sought to suggest a favorite thought of the author that she

Marcel he learned about "I–Thou" relationships, and from Maritain, artistic symbolism and the peculiar modern penchant for separating man's mind from his body.

It was not long after his release from the Connecticut sanatorium that he married. Six months later he and his bride entered the Catholic Church. He never did practice medicine. Instead, he decided to try his hand at writing. He produced two unpublished novels. Undismayed, he wrote a third, which was returned to him for further work. Over the next fourteen months he retooled the novel twice. It was finally published, although the publisher did little to promote it. Percy was forty-four at this time and going seemingly nowhere. Yet despite the cool treatment the publisher gave *The Moviegoer,* it was discovered and won for its author the highly prestigious National Book Award. Percy's patience not only paid off, it hit the jackpot.

Five novels followed, establishing Percy as one of the most important literary figures on the American scene. One literary critic said that "Percy ranks with Swift as that rare accomplished acrobat, the novelist who can balance interesting fiction with serious ideas." Another referred to him as "the satiric Dostoyevsky of the bayou."[3] In one of the foremost works about Percy—*Walker Percy: An American Search*—Robert Coles praised him for having "a sharp eye for all the pompous self-important and self-centered baloney that is eating away at American secular culture—its moral drift, its egoism, rootlessness and greed" and for being "onto both the liberals and the conservatives" and hitting "the blind spots in both camps".

---

expressed by the Greek words *en hypomene:* waiting in patience. See p. 51.

[3] "Walker Percy", *Contemporary Literary Criticism,* ed. D. G. Marowski (Detroit: Gage Research, 1991), vol. 65, p. 257.

Although the main theme of Percy's novels and essays is man's alienation from the familiar world of here and now, he was a gracious and genial man who was apparently cheerfully comfortable and quite at home in this world. He seemed to personify the Christian ideal of being *in* the world but not *of* the world.

He once gave a lecture at Cornell University on the Russian writer Anton Chekhov that drew an interesting parallel to his own personal odyssey. Chekhov was also a doctor who did not particularly like medicine and was also tubercular (he died at age forty-four). The title of Percy's presentation was "The Novelist, Diagnostician of the Contemporary Malaise". It was an exquisite summation of Percy's life: Dr. Walker Percy, the trained pathologist, applying his diagnostic skills to the troubled condition of modern man and, with the patience of a surgeon, writing his harsh prescription in graceful and moving prose.

When Percy died in May of 1990, Cleanth Brooks, literary critic and Yale University professor, said of him: "In losing Walker Percy, we have lost a remarkable figure in American literature, and a generous man. Some of us have lost a very kind and dear friend."[4]

Commentary

Patience allows us to maintain peace of mind in the midst of life's continuing anxieties. It permits us to persevere in directing our energies toward a positive goal despite persistent disappointments, restrictions, and hardships. It helps us to be composed in a crisis and to retain our equanimity in the face of the innumerable irritations that crop up from

[4] Ibid., p. 256.

day to day. Patience gives us the flexibility we need so that we can find worthwhile pursuits when other opportunities have been taken from us. Patience allows us to abide foolishness without growing angry and to endure tedium without becoming bored.

Contrary to popular sentiment, patience is not a passive virtue. Much inner strength is required not to become discouraged or give up when things are not going our way. A patient person is a man of substance, though it might be wise not to push him too far; "Beware the fury of a patient man", warned the poet Dryden.[5]

Patience, therefore, can be related to fortitude (or courage). Aristotle maintained that patience is so much like fortitude that she seems either her sister or her daughter. Patience is the calmer face of courage that proves itself over time. The patience of Job is one of the most moving testimonies we have of the indomitable power of the human spirit. Job illustrates the concentrated strength that patience demands. Not to be crushed under the weight of immense suffering and not to despair when suffering remains unrelieved epitomize the positive force of patience.

Enrico Caruso was the most admired Italian operatic singer of his time. In his repertoire, which included forty-three operas, he displayed a dramatic vocal technique that was unequalled in variety and scope. Yet his musical prowess may pale when contrasted with the patience and courage his mother must have possessed, for Enrico, the eighteenth child born to Mrs. Anna (Baldini) Caruso, was her first to survive infancy.[6]

Boethius (480–524) was a great scholar and a Roman

[5] John Dryden, *Absalom and Achitophel*, line 1005.
[6] *Dictionary of American Biography*, vol. 3, ed. Allen Johnson (New York: Charles Scribner's Sons, 1929), p. 549.

senator. When he fell from royal favor, he was imprisoned on trumped-up charges of treason and sentenced to death. During his two years of incarceration, he meditated on the ultimate issues of fate and destiny. Writing without benefit of a library, and relying on his well-cultivated memory, he wrote one of the enduring masterpieces of philosophical literature, *The Consolation of Philosophy.* Edward Gibbon, not always disposed to philosophy, found it "a golden volume . . . which claims incomparable merit from the barbarism of the times and the situation of the author".[7] King Alfred the Great (849–899) regarded it as one of his golden four of "the books most necessary for all men to know".[8] Boethius developed the thought and the personal conviction that "the only true joy is self-possession in the face of adversity."[9] He aimed at cultivating through patience a temperament that no trials or tribulations could shatter.

Patience can be undaunted. Edwin Kowalik said that he knew he was destined to play the piano the first time he touched one. But he became permanently blind as the result of a fall when he was seven. After learning music in Braille, he lost his memory in an automobile crash. He recovered his memory and went on to become an internationally acclaimed concert pianist. He also transcribed into the Braille system the complete works of Frederic Chopin.[10]

[7] Quoted by Daniel J. Boorstin in *The Creators* (New York: Random House, 1992), pp. 235–36.

[8] Ibid., p. 237.

[9] Boethius, *The Consolation of Philosophy,* trans. Richard Green (Indianapolis, Ind.: Bobbs-Merrill, 1962), p. 27.

[10] Hanna Czuma, "Maestro Brings Music and Joy out of Darkness", *The Catholic Register,* January 16, 1993, p. 12.

Patience is also hopeful. It sits on the rock of fortitude, but its gaze is toward the skies. "How poor are they that have not patience!" wrote Shakespeare, "What wound did ever heal but by degree?"[11] There are times when all we can do is wait and hope, circumstances when patience and time can do far more good than power and passion. In this regard, patience is also sensible and practical, as a Dutch proverb advises: "A handful of patience is worth a bushel of brains."

Patience is modest and unassuming. On July 23, 1863, Sonya Tolstaya wrote a single underscored word in her diary—*"Patience"*.[12] She knew at this moment, at nineteen years of age and in the first year of her marriage, that her husband was incapable of tending to practical matters and as a consequence, full responsibility for managing the vast household in Yasnaya Polyana and Moscow would fall to her. Little did she realize at that time how much more patience she would need throughout her forty-eight-year marriage that produced sixteen children and trials that would test the patience of a saint.

The following year Count Tolstoy began working on *War and Peace.* For the next twenty years, until her daughter shared this chore with her, Sonya made fair copies of her husband's work.[13] It is reported that she copied the entire manuscript of *War and Peace* seven times,[14] a task made

[11] William Shakespeare, *Othello*, 2.3.379.

[12] O. A. Golinenko et al. (eds.), *The Diaries of Sofia Tolstaya*, trans. Cathy Porter (London: Jonathan Cape, 1985), p. 22.

[13] Louise Smoluchowski, *Lev and Sonya: The Story of the Tolstoy Marriage* (London: Sidgwick and Jackson, 1987), p. 68.

[14] Ibid.: "Once she [Sonya] said that she had copied *War and Peace*

even more daunting because her husband's writing was barely legible and scrawled with erasures and lines of script that often crisscrossed in every direction. Yet she rarely knocked on his door for help and never complained. The novel was barely half-finished when Sonya began to realize that it would be a truly extraordinary work, and took great joy in performing her modest role as copyist. Still, patience has its rewards. Tolstoy was profoundly influenced by his wife's virtuous example. Sonya was, without exaggeration, the good wife of Scripture.[15] Though she did remain in the background, personally, her influence can be seen in many of her husband's works. As one researcher has observed: "Sonya made her contribution to all of Leo's great women characters."[16]

Finally, patience is ever alert to new vistas. When one door is closed, patience finds a new one to open. If something appears without fanfare, patience will take the time to find its inner glory. When the moment seems unpromising, patience will discover some surprising benefaction. As the symbolist poet Paul Valéry states:

> Patience, patience,
> Patience in the blue sky!
> Each atom of silence

---

seven times." See also, John Stewart Collis, *Marriage and Genius* (London: Cassell, 1963), p. 138: "[Sonya was] so appreciative of his work that nothing gave her greater happiness than the copying out of *War and Peace* seven times."

[15] Karl Stern, *The Flight from Woman* (New York: Farrar, Straus, and Giroux, 1965), p. 176.

[16] Smoluchowski, op. cit., p. 69.

is the chance of a ripe fruit!
The glad surprise will come;
A dove, a stirring of the breeze,
The gentlest shaking,
A woman's touch
will bring rain
When we shall fall on our knees.[17]

[17] Quoted in Gabriel Marcel, *Homo Viator,* trans. Emma Craufurd (New York: Harper and Row, 1962), p. 264. "Patience, patience, / Patience dans l'azur! / Chaque atome de silence / Est la chance d'un fruit mur! / Viendra l'heureuse surprise; / Une colombe la brise, / L'ébranlement le plus doux, / Une femme qui s'appuie, / Feront tomber cette pluie / Où l'on se jette à genoux."

PIETY

IN THE SPRING of 1981, the distinguished sociologist George Gilder had been asked to give a speech to the forty-fifth reunion of his father's graduating class of Harvard University, Gilder's own alma mater. Gilder's father had been a bomber-pilot and was killed in the Second World War. Gilder had not known his father at all. He was reported to have done a great deal of writing, but the only piece familiar to Gilder was a once-famous front-page editorial he had written for Harvard's *Crimson* on the occasion of Franklin Roosevelt's arrival at the University for its tercentenary celebration in 1936. He was intrigued by the olympian tone of its closing exhortation: "Let the presence of this man in the White House at the time of our great tercentenary celebration serve as a useful antidote to the natural over-emphasis on Harvard's successes."

The very day after Gilder received the first bound pages of his work on economics and the importance of family moral values, *Wealth and Poverty,* he was informed that a large box of his father's papers had been discovered in his uncle's basement. At the top of the box was a 175-page manuscript on economics that he had been working on when he died. One of its themes was the importance of what he called "intangible capital". It corresponded almost perfectly with Gilder's own thesis in *Wealth and Poverty,* namely, that the driving force of a free economy is not material resources or even physical capital but what he refers to as "the metaphysical capital of family and faith".

The manuscript confirmed a deep sense Gilder had carried throughout his youth that he was linked in an almost mystical way to this father he had never known. Family, for Gilder, is not an arbitrary accident of parental pressure and example that ends with emancipation from the household. Its influence is not limited by genes or home environment. It transcends distance and even death.

"My father taught me no economics," Gilder writes, "and Harvard taught me scarcely more in the one introductory course I took and barely passed. Yet discovering the literature of the subject in my fortieth year, I tapped a new source of creativity and intellectual power that I never imagined I possessed. I like to think some of that inspiration came from the young man in khaki in the war against the Nazis who left forever behind him a two-year-old boy and an unfinished text of economics in a box."[1]

Most of the achievement in the world reflects the force of family. Gilder confesses that it took him most of the twenty years after he had graduated from Harvard to recover the wisdom of his youth: "the beliefs in God and family", he writes, "taught to me, chiefly by my mother, as I was growing up on a farm in Massachusetts."[2] He was now preparing to address his father's graduating class of 1936 and to speak to them about the indispensable role of "intangible capital" and the irreplaceability of marriage and morality, family and faith.

This mystical link, transcending the antipodes of life and death, between a father and his son is no more powerful

[1] George Gilder, *Men and Marriage* (Gretna, La.: Pelican, 1992), p. 193.
[2] Ibid., p. 191.

than that between a mother and her daughter, as the following story will attest.

Rose Tavino Manes was fast asleep, one August night in 1986, when she was suddenly awakened by her mother's voice. Since her mother had returned to God five years earlier, the experience was particularly startling. Nonetheless, the voice was both clear and compelling: *"Rosa, è scritt? è scritt?"* (or, in more conventional Italian, *"Rosa, hai scritto? hai scritto?* [Rose, have you written? Have you written?]").[3]

Upon hearing her mother speak so distinctly and insistently, Rose had a vision portraying a beautiful adolescent carrying a jug of water on her head. Simultaneously a flash of light illuminated the room with such brilliance it brought Rose to her feet. She proceeded at once to her typewriter and, over the course of the next few hours, produced an astonishing fifty pages of copy. As she would later attest, "The words seemed to flow directly from Heaven."[4]

The following morning she handed these pages to her own daughter, Palmina, who had been especially close to Rose's mother. Instinctively, Palmina recognized that she was reading a story about her beloved grandmother, though she could not believe that her mother had produced it in so short a time during the previous night. She urged her mother to write more. Prodded by both her mother and her daughter, Rose obliged. Over the next three years she researched and completed what is now a published novel, *Prima Vera: Springtime,* incorporating, as chapters seven through fourteen, essentially without alteration, the initial fifty pages she had written on that memorable August

[3] "Passing Along Family History", *Fra noi: Chicagoland's Italian American Voice,* March 1992, p. 30. The voice spoke in a dialect: *"Rosa, e scritt, e scritt?"*

[4] Correspondence from Rose T. Manes, July 27, 1994.

night. In her own opinion, these pages have a descriptive beauty that surpasses what is contained in any of the other chapters.

Prima Vera—which means "first truth", "first wedding ring", and the "first greens" that go into a sumptuous dish called *pasta primavera,* as well as "springtime"—spans eight decades and recounts the continuity and perpetual renewal of an Italian family and immigrant children and grandchildren as they make their transition from the mountains of the old country to the teaming cities of America. It is an inspiring and heartwarming story of the eternal spring of hope that holds not only successive generations of an Italian family together but all families as well.[5]

Commentary

Piety is not a superficial show of religiosity. Rather, it is a profound respect for the forces that preceded us and brought us into being. It is reverence for God, nature, and parents. By means of piety, a person remains united with what is good in his past, what is valuable and helpful in his tradition. As Tevya explains in *Fiddler on the Roof,* without tradition we do not know what is expected of us, and thus we become as vulnerable to a fall as a fiddler on a roof. Piety enables us to honor tradition in the Chestertonian sense as the "democracy of the dead".

The German word for piety is *pietät,* derived from the Latin *pietas.* One German translator, however, realizing

[5] Rose Tavino Manes, *Prima Vera: Springtime* (Fort Lauderdale, Fla.: Ashley Books, 1991). In the acknowledgement, the author expresses her "deep sense of gratitude" to her parents, particularly to her mother, "who always urged me to write".

that the essential meaning of *pietas* was in danger of being lost forever, coined the following word in order to preserve its original meaning: *Blutpflichtverbundenheit,* which literally means, despite its awkwardness, "blood-duty-connectedness". Piety is based on the realization that there is a connection or continuity between God and creatures, ancestors and descendents, parents and children. The virtue of piety involves the appropriate respect a person should have in honoring what came before him, initiating and shaping his life. Through piety, he does not stand alone but affirms the role he plays in the continuum of time. The man of piety affirms the good of the past and the good of the future because he is profoundly united with both. His piety is a great source of hope, because he knows that, since he does not act alone, a momentary setback in his own life may bring about a later success in those who come after him.

Socrates was a man of piety. In the Platonic dialogue *Euthyphro,* he meets a man who is bent on having his own father put to death. Socrates engages Euthyphro in a long conversation about virtue and morality. The subtleties of Socrates' line of reasoning, for the most part, elude Euthyphro, whose own ideas seem to flow, not from anything respectful of the past, but from his own excessive preoccupation with himself. Euthyphro impiously asserts that something is holy, not because it really is holy, but only because he says it is. Euthyphro is enamored more by power than by piety.

Boccaccio, who wrote a biography of Dante, tells a story about the great poet that would have very much pleased Socrates. Dante had bequeathed to the world one of the great glories of literature: *The Divine Comedy.* But at the time of his death in 1321, the last thirteen cantos of the final part of his epic, the "Paradiso", were nowhere to be found. Despairing admirers came to the point where they asked his sons Jacopo and Piero, both "rhymers", to complete their father's work. But, as Boccaccio reports, a fortuitous miracle made this unnecessary. One night, in the ninth month after Dante's death, while Jacopo di Dante was asleep:

> His father had appeared to him, clothed in the purest white, and his face resplendent with an extraordinary light. . . . Jacopo asked him if he lived, and . . . Dante replied: "Yes, but in the true life, not our life." Then Jacopo asked him if he had completed his work before passing into the true life, and . . . what had become of that part of it which was missing. . . . To this Dante seemed to answer: "Yes, I finished it."[6]

While still in the vision, Dante took his son by the hand and led him to a room. Touching one of the walls, he said, "What you have sought for so much is here." The next morning before dawn, Jacopo went to the room his father had designated and found, in a hidden recess, the missing cantos "all mouldy from the dampness of the walls, and had they remained there longer, in a little while they would have crumbled away."[7]

The German poet Jean Paul Richter once said that "The words a father speaks to his children in the privacy of the home are not overheard at the time, but as in whispering galleries, they will be heard at the end and by posterity."

---

[6] Daniel J. Boorstin, *The Creators* (New York: Random House, 1992), p. 263. The passage is the translation of F. J. Bunbury.

[7] Ibid. Ironically, when Dorothy Sayers died before she could complete her translation of the *Divine Comedy,* exactly thirteen cantos remained.

The following two stories, from disparate fields—baseball and psychotherapy—demonstrate how diverse the fruits of piety can be.

On the very last game of the regular season, October 6, 1985, an aging knuckleball pitcher by the name of Phil Niekro led the New York Yankees to an 8 to 0 victory over the Toronto Blue Jays. At forty-six years of age, he became the oldest hurler ever to pitch a shutout in major league history. His win was also the three hundreth of his career, a feat that virtually guarantees election to baseball's Hall of Fame. What was most meaningful for Niekro that day, however, was not his four-hit shutout or three hundredth win but the fact that his father was released from intensive care.

Immediately after the game, dodging reporters, he flew to the hospital where his dad was recovering and placed in his hand the ball he had thrown to strike out the final batter—the very hand that many years before had shown him how to throw a knuckleball. Papa Niekro had been an amateur pitcher. When an injury to his arm dashed any hopes of ever making it to the big leagues, he learned a pitch that produces relatively little strain on the arm. He taught his two sons how to throw the knuckler and, between them, "Knuxie" and his brother Joe became the winningest brother tandem ever to pitch in the major leagues. But it wasn't the individual achievements of either Phil or Joe that were most important. It was a family triumph, and papa Niekro shared in his sons' accomplishments as much as if not more than they did themselves.

Shortly before the United States entered World War II, Viktor Frankl was called to the American Consulate in Vienna to receive his immigration visa. His parents fully expected him to leave Austria as soon as he acquired his visa so that he could go to the United States and disseminate his newly developed theory of logotherapy.

For Frankl himself, however, the decision to leave Austria was problematic. The prospect of leaving his parents beset him. He knew that because they were Jewish, they were in constant danger of being taken away to a concentration camp. It was the kind of dilemma that left Frankl hoping for a sign from heaven. The most difficult moral decisions human beings are compelled to make are often not between good and evil but between two goods that are in conflict with each other. It was then that Frankl noticed a piece of marble lying on a table at his parents' home. When he asked his father about it, the latter explained that he had found it on the site where the National Socialists had burned to the ground Vienna's largest synagogue. It was the part of the tablets that contained the Ten Commandments. The piece displayed one engraved and gilded Hebrew letter, an abbreviation for the commandment "Honor thy father and thy mother, that thy days may be long upon the land." Frankl took this as his sign, stayed with his parents, and allowed his American visa to lapse.[8]

When the time was propitious, Frankl came to America and successfully launched his new and yet ageless concept of logotherapy—healing the soul through examining one's reason for living. It is no coincidence that Frankl's logotherapy is steeped in piety. One can discover the meaning of one's life only by reflecting on one's origins. To answer the question, "Where am I going?" one must first stop to answer "Where have I come from?"

[8] Viktor Frankl, *Psychotherapy and Existentialism: Selected Papers on Logotherapy* (New York: Simon and Schuster, 1967), p. 34.

PRUDENCE

THROUGHOUT HISTORY, the customary way of teaching morality has not been through philosophical treatises on the nature of virtue. It is a rare individual who derives any personal benefit from a strictly intellectual approach to morality. If virtue was not communicated through the good example of respected people, it was usually conveyed through stories, folktales, or fables. One of the more ambitious, dramatic, and powerful ways of imparting morality is through opera. This vehicle has great moral potential inasmuch as it represents the synthesis of several arts: singing, orchestration, dialogue, poetry, acting, costuming, staging, and direction. "Grand Opera" is particularly well suited to convey a moral message, at times with almost irresistible force. Giuseppe Verdi's *Il Trovatore* (The troubadour) is a case in point.[1] The opera's story is a series of tragedies that flow from a prejudicial view of human beings that is fundamentally unrealistic in its conception and leads to actions that are profoundly imprudent.

The opera is set in fifteenth-century Aragon at a time when wandering singers, known as troubadours, are in flower. The Count di Luna has condemned a gypsy woman to be burned at the stake on the spurious grounds that she

---

[1] *The Definitive Kobbé's Opera Book* (New York: G. P. Putnam's Sons, 1987), pp. 454–62. The libretto, written by Salvatore Cammarano, is taken from the drama *Il Trovatore,* by Antonio Garcia Gutiérez.

has bewitched the younger of his two sons, causing him to fall ill. The woman is a victim of the Count's prejudice as well as his superstition. As the woman is about to die, she enjoins her daughter, Azucena, to avenge her. Azucena accepts her mother's dying command, kidnaps the Count's younger son, and carries him off to hurl him into the furnace while the flames are still raging over the spot where her mother has perished. Her mother's words, "Avenge thou me!", resound in her already disordered mind, blinding her to what she is doing. As a result, she mistakenly incinerates her own child, who had also been with her.

Azucena is horrified beyond words when she realizes what she has done. She decides to keep the Count's child and raise him as her own, but with the thought that through him she might one day wreak vengeance upon his kin. Manrico grows to manhood and becomes strong, capable, and handsome. He enters a tournament and wins. The beautiful Duchess Leonora crowns him victor and the two fall passionately in love with each other. Thereafter, Manrico the Troubadour returns nightly to serenade his beloved with haunting love songs.

The love between Leonora and Manrico belongs to a higher, more human order than the vengeance and rage that blind others to the nature of their own self-destructive actions. The plot thickens when Manrico's older brother, who became the Count di Luna after his father's death, also falls in love with Leonora. When Leonora is falsely informed that her Manrico has been killed in battle, she decides to become a nun. Just prior to the moment when she is to take her vows, Manrico arrives and takes her away with him, a maneuver that his older brother and rival had planned to execute.

The Count captures Azucena, charges her with the murder of his younger brother, and sentences her to be burned at the stake. Manrico rushes to rescue her but is also imprisoned by the Count and condemned to die. Leonora offers herself in marriage to the Count on the condition that he set her beloved Manrico free. When the Count accepts her offer, she takes a slow-working but deadly poison. Leonora dies saying farewell to Manrico: "Sooner than live another's bride, Near thee I prefer to die!"

Infuriated, the Count breaks his promise and executes Manrico. Azucena then seizes the opportunity to have her revenge by informing the Count that he has just murdered his own brother: "The victim was thy brother, Thou art avenged, O mother!"

The Count is completely devastated. He, too, like Azucena before him, has unwittingly slaughtered his own flesh and blood. Realizing that he will never know a moment's peace of mind as long as he lives, he curses his life as a fate worse than death.

Il Trovatore, apart from being a great opera, is a powerful morality play. The Count di Luna, an aristocrat, views Azucena's mother, a gypsy, as an inferior type of human being whose mere presence can bring harm to his son. As the story proceeds from this unrealistic assessment of the woman—what is more commonly known as prejudice—it illustrates the sorry chain of events that imprudence can set in motion. Imprudence is acting without regard for the knowledge needed to bring one's action into harmony with justice, fortitude, and temperance. Its essential defect lies in its narrowness, its gross insufficiency of pertinent and realistic information. Just as it is imprudent in a practical sense to drive a car at night without the headlights on, it is imprudent in a moral sense to act without using the light of reason. In short, "the prudent [man] looks where he is going."[2]

The Count di Luna acted imprudently when he acted on the assumption that the gypsy woman, merely because she was that, had somehow contaminated his son. Killing the woman logically bred in the daughter a seething desire for revenge. But her rage, in turn, produced blindness, which led to imprudence followed by inconsolable remorse and stronger vengeance. This concatenation of evils develops along a completely different plane of reality than does the love Manrico and Leonora have for each other and the love that develops between Azucena and her adopted son, Manrico (despite their difference in social standing). They differ from each other as vice does from virtue. Though love and virtue have the power to lead people away from corruption and vice, this does not happen in the tragedy of "The Troudadour".

Commentary

Prudence is "the charioteer of the virtues".[3] It steers other virtues, especially the other cardinal virtues—justice, fortitude, and temperance—in the right direction. Regrettably, however, as is the case with most virtues, this most eminent of practical virtues, this mold and mother of all other virtues, is often misunderstood.[4]

[2] Prov 14:15 (RSV).
[3] *Catechism of the Catholic Church,* 1806, p. 382. The notion of prudence as a "charioteer" (*auriga virtutum*) has roots in Plato's *Phaedrus* 246; 253c.
[4] Josef Pieper, *The Four Cardinal Virtues* (New York: Harcourt, Brace and World, 1965), p. 22.

Prudence is commonly mistaken for "cleverness". But cleverness is not a moral virtue. A person may use cleverness to avoid his moral obligations. He may cleverly avoid certain situations or decline to make statements that would oblige him to be just, courageous, or temperate. Cleverness in this regard may actually resemble cowardice more than true prudence, which courage presupposes. Nor does prudence have anything to do with being tactical, cunning, or sly. These are strategic qualities and are not intrinsically related to morality. A criminal cannot do without such qualities if he is to outwit the authorities and stay out of prison.

Prudence is the ability to be circumspect and decisive about an action so as to transform knowledge of reality into the realization of a good. A person sizes up a situation and, with the realistic knowledge he has gained thereby, proceeds to act for a good end. The decision to marry a particular person at a particular time demands a high degree of prudence. One should not walk into marriage blind. But more than that, when a person has enough knowledge of whatever is pertinent to his situation to make a prudent marital decision, he also welcomes the inevitable challenges that his marriage will introduce with regard to justice, fortitude, and temperance. If a person imprudently rushes into marriage, he is not prepared to be either just to or temperate with his partner, or to be courageous when difficult circumstances arise. Prudence is a particularly demanding virtue because it must anticipate the need for consequent virtues.

While one form of imprudence is impetuosity, recklessness, or precipitousness, another is irresoluteness, indecisiveness, or endless procrastination. Prudence demands knowledge of the facts, but it also requires coming to a decision. The person who thinks that indecisiveness is always a prudent way of playing things safe, shows no appreciation for what prudence entails. T. S. Eliot's Prufrock, who asks "Do I dare disturb the universe?" is exhibiting not prudence, but catatonia.[5] On the other hand, Eliot's opposite character, Sweeney, displays reckless imprudence when he consistently rushes into things without thinking.

In order to make a prudent decision, a person needs an open mind so as to assess the facts in an honest and undistorted manner. He is also assisted if he has considerable experience and a good memory that, as much as possible, accurately recalls that experience.

Prudence is rooted in an acceptance of reality. Therefore mere "good intentions" or "meaning well" do not provide an adequate basis for a truly prudent act. Prudence begins with the perception of what is really involved and culminates in choosing the right course of action. Consequently, prudence works very closely with moral conscience, which is an inclination to do good and to avoid evil. The word "conscience" is derived from *con-scientia* ("with knowledge"). Therefore, conscience, rightly considered, must always be intimately involved with knowledge. As the French playwright Paul Claudel has stated, conscience is "the patient beacon which does not delineate the future, but only the immediate". The prudent man knows what is at stake and therefore has an informed conscience. At the same time, he is guided by his conscience to choose what is good or to avoid what is evil. The good he chooses presupposes a corresponding knowledge of all the real elements that are relevant to his choice. Prudence is the power to make an enlightened choice that is consistent with conscience and directed toward a moral good.

[5] T. S. Eliot, "The Love Song of J. Alfred Prufrock".

One of the brightest, most original mathematicians of the nineteenth century was Evariste Galois. For reasons that are not exactly clear, he accepted a challenge to participate in a duel. Certain of his forthcoming death, Galois spent his final night writing out as much of his mathematical theories as time would permit: sixty pages in all, an algebraic treasure that would later establish him as a mathematician of permanent historical significance. He was found in a ditch the next morning with a bullet in his stomach and died shortly thereafter in a hospital. At the time of his death he was just twenty years of age. On the surface of things it appears that his decision to accept the duel (which was, in fact, illegal) and go to a certain death at such a tender age was surely imprudent.[6]

Mark Twain, who had a wonderful gift for combining humor with insight, once said that "It is by the goodness of God that in our country we have those three unspeakably precious things: freedom of speech, freedom of conscience, and the prudence never to practice either." Twain is playing on the ambiguity of the word "freedom", which often is taken to mean licence. It would be contrary to prudence to endorse a completely unprincipled, unregulated freedom of speech and freedom of conscience. In other words, it would be prudent to avoid mischief. But this is only half the work of prudence. Twain's witticism does not take into account the positive function of prudence, which is to choose what is good. Such a choice, in the final analysis, requires some measure of wisdom. Wisdom and prudence, consequently, differ only in degree, wisdom being nothing more than consummate prudence.

[6] Jane Muir, "Evariste Galois", in *Of Men and Numbers* (New York: Dell, 1961), p. 248.

REVERENCE

WILLIAM F. BUCKLEY was once asked who, among his numberless acquaintances, best combined the virtues of scholarship and saintliness. Buckley identified Gerhart Niemeyer, but stipulated that had he been asked prior to coming to know the distinguished political science professor at the University of Notre Dame, who was ordained to the Episcopal priesthood and then later converted to Catholicism, he would have named Whittaker Chambers. Philosopher Sidney Hook said of Chambers that he not only wrote "one of the most significant autobiographies of the twentieth century" but, as a gesture of uncommon altruism, "committed moral suicide to atone for the guilt of our generation". Chambers' life, not only because it portrayed a man of scholarship and saintliness, but because of the way its unexpected twists and turns shook the moral and political world of two continents, would have been too improbable for fiction.

He was born in 1901 and grew up in Lynbrook, Long Island. The one book that had the greatest impact on him during his formative years was Victor Hugo's *Les Misérables,* which he read many times in its entirety.[1] This work, which he referred to as "the Bible of my boyhood", taught him that Christianity and revolution are "two seemingly irreconcilable things". After reading Lenin

[1] Whittaker Chambers, *Witness* (New York: Random House, 1952), p. 134.

196

at Columbia University, Chambers went to England, where he joined the Communist party and became chief editor of the *Daily Worker*. An indefatigable propagandist, he found time to translate a number of French and German books into English. In the 1930s he served as a courier in the Soviet espionage apparatus in Washington, D.C. In 1938 he broke with the Communist party. In his autobiography, he points to two decisive moments in his life that led him to lose faith in the Communist ideology.

"For one of us to have a child", his brother had said to him, "would be a crime against nature." Though he longed for children, Chambers agreed with his brother. It was considered morally wrong for a professional revolutionist in the Communist party to have children. They would only hamper or distract his more important work. Even as an underground Communist, he took it for granted that children were out of the question.

Abortion, therefore, was commonplace in party life. There were Communist doctors who rendered the service for a small fee. Abortion, which Chambers would later look upon with "physical horror", he then regarded, like all Communists, as a mere physical manipulation. When his wife became pregnant, she made it known to him that she wanted the child. "Dear heart," she said to him in a pleading voice, "we couldn't do that awful thing to a little baby, not to a little baby, dear heart." [2] The edifice that he had established through many years of Communist involvement suddenly crumbled at the touch of a child. The baby was born, and her parents named her Ellen. "If the points on the long course of my break with Communism could be retraced," Chambers wrote, "that is probably one of them—

[2] Ibid., p. 325.

not at the level of the conscious mind, but at the level of unconscious life."[3]

The second decisive moment occurred when his daughter was seated in her high chair. He was watching her smear porridge over her face when his eye came to rest on the delicate convolutions of her ear—"those intricate, perfect ears". Then it occurred to him that those ears could not have been created by any chance alignment of atoms. They could not possibly be explained by tenets of dialectical materialism. They could have been created only by design. The implication was inexorable: Design presupposed God. "At that moment," he wrote, "the finger of God was first laid upon my forehead."[4]

Chambers begins his autobiography by addressing his two children. He reminds them of what they learned from their youthful experiences, the two most important things human beings ever know: the wonder of life and the wonder of the universe. He urges them to continue to look at the wonder of life that exists within the wonder of the universe with "reverence and awe—that reverence and awe that has died out of the modern world and been replaced by man's monkeylike amazement at the cleverness of his own inventive brain."[5]

Chambers was led through his own reverence—for life in the womb and the miraculous convolutions of his daughter's ear—back to his Christian roots. He realized that he had been an involuntary witness to God's grace. From his new perspective he discovered that *Les Misérables* offered a Christian and not a Communist message. When he reexamined the last line of Dante's "Inferno"—"And so

[3] Ibid., p. 326.
[4] Ibid., p. 16.
[5] Ibid., p. 19.

we emerged again to see the stars"[6]—which, he said, is also the last line of Marx's *Das Kapital,* he understood that the object of his faith had changed from a utopian future with men to an eternal life with God.

Chambers began working with *Time* magazine in 1939 and soon became one of the organization's most brilliant and controversial writers. He rose to the level of senior editor, a position only seven men enjoyed at that time. In 1948 he testified before the House Committee on Un-American Activities about his earlier Communist connections and identified Alger Hiss, a former State Department official, as one of his Communist associates who had supplied him with documents to be turned over to Communist agents. Hiss sued, but Chambers produced microfilm copies of the documents in question—the so-called "pumpkin papers"—which he had hidden in a hollowed out pumpkin on his farm.[7] Hiss was indicted for perjury, convicted, and sent to prison.

The Chambers-Hiss affair was intensely controversial. When Chambers published his autobiography in 1952, *Witness,* his powerful prose and candid revelations gave the controversy fresh impetus. Chambers viewed the issue as a clash of faiths, between ideology and true religion. But this clash subsumed another conflict, one more fundamental and universal, namely, the one between belief in a utopian dream of future men and reverence for the individual persons one meets in the present.

---

[6] "E quindi uscimmo a riveder le stelle."
[7] Chambers, *Witness,* p. 539.

Commentary

Professors Dietrich and Alice von Hildebrand state, "Reverence is *the* attitude which can be designated as the mother of all moral life, for in it man first takes a position toward the world which opens his spiritual eyes and enables him to grasp values."[8]

It is commonplace in a materialistic and hedonistic world for self-absorption to displace a spirit of reverence. When this occurs, the moral life is strangled at its very roots. The contemporary world speaks glibly of the importance of having an "open mind", but it rarely encourages an attitude of reverence that is, in fact, an attitude of open-mindedness toward objective truth. Reverence, therefore, is the mother of the moral life inasmuch as it allows a person to recognize what is good and worthy of honor. "To whom will the sublime beauty of a sunset or a Ninth Symphony of Beethoven reveal itself", ask the von Hildebrands, "but to him who approaches it reverently and unlocks his heart to it?"[9]

Beethoven's home in Bonn, Germany, has been converted into a memorial museum. In one of the rooms, roped off from the reach of eager hands, sits the piano upon which the master composed many of his great works. A student from Vassar College, visiting with a party of American students, looked at the instrument rapturously and asked the guard if she might play the piano for a brief moment. Allowing himself to be influenced by her generous tip, the guard granted permission, and the student proceeded to strum a few bars of the Moonlight Sonata.

[8] Dietrich and Alice von Hildebrand, *The Art of Living* (Chicago: Franciscan Press, 1965), p. 4.

[9] Ibid., p. 7.

After finishing her mini-recital, she commented to the guard, "I suppose all the great pianists who have come here at one time or another have played on it." The guard remarked, "No, Miss, Paderewski was here two years ago but said he was not worthy to touch it."[10]

Reverence allows us to escape the dreary preoccupation of being a truncated self inhabiting the cramped world of self-interest. We need to be in touch with riches that lie outside of ourselves in order to be able to endure ourselves. As Dostoevsky stated, "A man who bows down to nothing, can never bear the burden of himself."[11] Reverence expands, self-interest contracts. For this reason, Plato advised, "We should leave our children rich, not in gold but in reverence."[12]

An irreverent attitude, although popular, especially among comics, is actually a weakness. The practice of jeering at traditional values that are grounded in an objective order reveals a kind of spiritual blindness, a character trait that is hardly enviable.

There are two forms of irreverence. The first involves pride. In this case a person is riveted to himself in such a way that his ruling concern is whether or not something will enhance his prestige, bring him honor, and make him famous. Such an individual suspects nothing of the breadth and depth of the world. He has no concern for values themselves. He is not concerned about justice or sacrifice or dedication to objective values. His pride is the absorbing center of his life.

The second form of irreverence springs from lust or

[10] Edmund Fuller (ed.), *Thesaurus of Anecdotes* (New York: Crown Publishers, 1942), p. 68.
[11] Fyodor Dostoevsky, *A Raw Youth* (London: Heineman, 1916).
[12] Plato *Laws* 5.729c.

selfish desire, what the Scholastics referred to as "concupiscence". Such a person is essentially concerned about whether or not things are pleasing or agreeable to him. He is equally blind to the inherent value of things and does not view anything with calm disinterest. He uses people for himself rather than honoring them for their own value. His motivation is primarily, "What's in it for me?"

The irreverent attitude, since it is rooted in isolated self-interest, not only is an impediment to moral growth but also inhibits the ability to love another person. For love is the positive and affirming response on the part of the lover to the value or preciousness he finds in the loved one. An inability to recognize this value precludes the possibility of love. One of the surest signs of the dawn of love is the concomitant experience of the beloved's worth and the lover's unworthiness.

Pascal once remarked that "the greatness of man is great in so far as he realizes that he is wretched."[13] The virtue of reverence allows us to appreciate great things that originate from sources wholly outside ourselves. Paradoxically, reverence, which centers, not on the greatness of ourselves, but on something other than ourselves, is the truest sign of our own greatness. There can be no realization or appreciation of greatness, within or beyond the self, apart from the combination of reverence and humility.

"Christianity is strange", remarked Pascal. "It bids man recognize that he is base, even abominable; it also bids him desire to be like God."[14] Humility and reverence serve as counterweights for each other. Wretchedness alone encourages despair, whereas mere reverence for great things encour-

[13] Blaise Pascal, *Pensées,* trans. Martin Turnell (New York: Harper and Row, 1962), p. 94.
[14] Ibid., p. 251.

ages pride. Man has a dual capacity for being deprived of grace: *despair,* which results from thinking in too lowly a way about himself; and *pride,* which comes from thinking about himself in too lofty a manner. The combination of humility and reverence allows him to know his greatness without succumbing to pride while, at the same time, to know his humanness without falling into despair.

Reverence is a latent and delicate power that requires much nurturing. Aristotle alluded to the fact that, in general, people are more easily swayed by fear than inspired by reverence.[15] By the same token, he went on to say, they are more apt to refrain from wrongdoing because they fear punishment rather than because they perceive the inherent wickedness of their deeds. The distinguished jurist Oliver Wendell Holmes, Sr., stated the matter more poetically when he wrote: "I have in my heart a small, shy plant called reverence; I cultivate that on Sunday mornings." This sentiment would no doubt have won the admiration of the German poet Goethe, for whom "the soul of the Christian religion is reverence."

"The world will never starve for want of wonders", wrote G. K. Chesterton, "but only for want of wonder." The reverent person will never run out of wondrous experiences, because he is in tune with the cosmos. But the irreverent person, who lacks the cultivated capacity to appreciate how wondrous the world really is, will find life empty. His lack of reverence will, in effect, banish all wonder from his life.

---

[15] Aristotle *Nicomachean Ethics* 10.

SINCERITY

JOHN PEYTON, the eldest of sixteen children, raised his five daughters and four sons in the same three-room thatched cottage on a farm in County Mayo, Ireland, where his father and his father before him had raised their families. From the time of their wedding night, John and his wife, Mary, knelt each evening before the hearth and prayed the Rosary. One by one, their children joined them until all eleven were reciting together this centuries-old prayer. The family Rosary was such a normal and accepted practice in the Peyton household that Patrick, the sixth child, was "thunderstruck" the day he discovered that it was not said in every Catholic home in his neighborhood.[1]

Life on the Peyton farm—fourteen acres of stony land on Ireland's western coast—was particularly hard because the land had to be worked without benefit of machinery. The family's economic situation was equally hard, driving the two eldest daughters to find employment in the United States so they could send money back home. In 1928, at the age of nineteen, it was time for Patrick to leave home and head for America. He was accompanied by his brother Tom.

Patrick and his brother eventually entered the seminary to study for the priesthood of the Congregation of the

[1] Patrick Peyton, C.S.C., *All for Her* (Hollywood, Calif.: Family Theater Publications, 1973), p. 21.

Holy Cross. All seemed well until Patrick began coughing up blood. Soon the coughing progressed to hemorrhaging. On one occasion the hemorrhaging was so bad that his examining physician did not think Patrick would survive the night. The diagnosis was "an advanced tuberculosis of the right upper lobe, with consolidation and a small cavity." In 1938, antibiotic treatment for tuberculosis had not been discovered. Treatment was virtually limited to diet and rest.

Peyton spent several months flat on his back. But his condition continued to worsen. Three medical doctors proposed a desperate and dangerous procedure. They would remove several ribs and break several others over the course of three major operations in order to make the shoulder blade fall in and give the diseased lung the rest it needed. The procedure would be a mutilation of Patrick's body and would leave him handicapped for life, even if it worked.[2] The doctors had already despaired of a normal recovery.

When Patrick was at his lowest ebb, his former ethics teacher at Notre Dame visited him. The visit was the turning point. In Peyton's autobiography, he refers to Father Hagerty as having made the "decisive contribution in what I regard as the supreme crisis and turning point of my life".[3]

There was a genuineness, a sincerity about Father Cornelius J. Hagerty that was unmistakable. As Peyton said about him: "Here was a man who would never wear a false face. He would say what he believed regardless of the consequences."[4] It was precisely Hagerty's sincerity that dis-

[2] Ibid., p. 53.
[3] Ibid., p. 9.
[4] Ibid., p. 55.

posed Peyton to take seriously what his old philosophy professor had to tell him. "Our Lady will be as good to you as you think she is. If you think she is a fifty per-center, that is what she will be; if you think she is a hundred per-center, she will be for you a hundred per-center. No one of us ever does as much as he is capable of doing. We always fall short, stopping on the near side of our total effort." Peyton was startled to be addressed in so forthright a manner. Hagerty went on: "Even Our Lord and Our Lady do not do as much as they could do, but the reason is that we think they are not able. We limit them by the extent of our faith."[5]

Having been reminded of his own faith and the power potential he already believed was contained in sincere prayer, Peyton prayed to our Lady with renewed confidence. Six days after Father Hagerty's visit, "the fog lifted." Two weeks later, the doctors were astonished to find that the pernicious fluid was gone, and they confessed that they had no way of accounting for the sudden improvement in Peyton's condition. The cure was total, and the malady never recurred. Peyton reflected on all those Rosaries he had recited with the other ten members of his family back in Ireland. Why should they not have paid a handsome dividend? He felt like a man who had paid insurance on his house and, now that the house had burned down, had come to collect his claim.[6]

Convinced that his sudden and scientifically inexplicable recovery was due to the intercession of Mary, he decided to devote the rest of his life to the promotion of the Rosary as a form of family prayer. He was now (as was his brother Tom) a priest. Although he had no idea how he

[5] Ibid., p. 56.
[6] Ibid., p. 57.

would begin spreading devotion to the Rosary, things began falling into place with providential inevitability. Movie stars such as Bing Crosby, Loretta Young, Maureen O'Hara, Jack Haley, Irene Dunne, and Jimmy Durante were most helpful. Bishops lent their support as did university personnel. The Family Rosary Crusade was airborne. Peyton carried his message that "the family that prays together stays together" throughout the world both in person and through the media. In addition to founding the Family Rosary Crusade, he established the Family Theater for television, which produced *The Joyful Hour* and *The Triumphant Hour,* a full-length movie (*The Redeemer*), and a shorter film (*The Promise*), the *Marian Hour* for radio, and the *Family Rosary Newspaper.*

In 1961 he addressed a gathering of 550,000 people in San Francisco's Golden Gate Park. That same year he spoke to 600,000 people in Caracas, Venezuela. The following year he prayed the Rosary before 1,500,000 in Rio de Janeiro, Brazil. His message, like that of his role model, Father Hagerty, was always one of utmost sincerity and genuineness.[7] He continued to bring his message—our Lady's message—to the four corners of the world for more than fifty years. "Prayer is God's weakness and my strength", he would say. "God wants to be invited into our homes so he can live there."[8]

---

[7] The author met Father Peyton on two occasions (in 1961 in North Easton, Mass., and thirty years later in Chicago) and does not recall having met anyone more utterly genuine and sincere.

[8] Raymond J. Cassel, "My Favorite Priest: Father Patrick Peyton, C.S.C.", *Homiletic and Pastoral Review,* October 1992, pp. 70–71. See also *Our Sunday Visitor,* August 1991.

Commentary

The word "sincere" comes from the Latin, *sincerus* which means "sound", "whole", "pure", "genuine", or "unmixed". It probably does not derive from *sine* (without) and *cera* (wax), although the story associated with this purported etymology is both endearing and illuminating.

When noblemen used messengers to send their letters, they would seal the envelope and then impress their signet into the sealing wax. If a courier was entirely trustworthy, a nobleman might send his mail "without wax", or unsealed. Sincerity in this sense refers to an attitude that is entirely open, one in which there is no barrier that would separate what is on the outside from the contents within.[9]

A person who displays sincerity in this sense is a most attractive figure. We like a person who has this kind of openness, reliability, and spontaneity. We find the tormented soul who is still searching for himself, or the man of obvious duplicity, far less engaging. In Shakespeare's *Two Gentlemen of Verona,* Julia rhapsodizes over her beloved Proteus, since she believes his "thousand oaths" and "ocean of tears" are utterly sincere:

> His words are bonds, his oaths are oracles;
> His love sincere, his thoughts immaculate;
> His tears pure messengers sent from his heart;
> His heart as far from fraud as heaven from earth.[10]

What poor Julia does not know at the time is how fickle and deceitful her suitor really is. He seemed to be sincere, but, as most of us know, sincerity is the easiest virtue to

[9] At least one etymologist of dubious reputation has signed his name "Yours waxlessly".

[10] William Shakespeare, *Two Gentlemen of Verona,* 2.7.76.

counterfeit. "It is often said it is no matter what man believes if he is only sincere", writes Henry Ward Beecher. "But let a man sincerely believe that seed planted without ploughing is as good as with; that January is as favorable for seed-sowing as April; and that cockle seed will produce as good a harvest as wheat, and is it so?"

Sincerity is probably the easiest virtue to dissimulate. To the question "Is there any 'sin' in 'sincere'?", the answer is a qualified "yes", the qualification being that the sincerity has nothing to do with the truth. One of Hitler's early followers, after hearing the *Führer* for the first time, had this to say: "I was a man of thirty-two, weary of disgust and disillusionment, a wanderer seeking a cause; a patriot without a channel for his patriotism, a yearner after the heroic without a hero. The intense will of the man, the passion of his sincerity, seemed to flow from him into me. I experienced an exaltation that could be likened only to religious conversion."[11]

Sincerity is "the most dangerous virtue",[12] as someone has said, because it can combine a natural attractiveness with a lethal seductiveness. The world of publicity— advertizing, propaganda, gossip—operates with the glow of sincerity and the almost complete absence of truth. Yet it is immensely successful because its facade of sincerity always manages to evoke in the masses at least some emotional response, however shallow that response may be. As face-to-face relationships diminish in an increasingly technologized society, it becomes easier for people to lie to each other. The "dangerous virtue" of sincerity, or vice, rather, induces

[11] T. L. Jarman, *The Rise and Fall of Nazi Germany* (New York: Signet, 1961), p. 97.

[12] James Schall, "On the Most Dangerous Virtue", *Review for Religious,* November 1974, p. 1301.

moral paralysis. Such "sincerity" asks of a person only that he be himself, that is, remain completely unreformed and serenely indifferent to the circumstances that surround him. In Walker Percy's award-winning novel *The Moviegoer,* the author has the protagonist's aunt expatiate on what is wrong with the contemporary world: "Our national character stinks to high heaven. But we are kinder than ever. No prostitute ever responded with a quicker spasm of sentiment when our hearts are touched. Nor is there anything new about thievery, lewdness, lying, adultery. What is new is that in our time liars and thieves and harlots and adulterers wish also to be congratulated and are congratulated by the great public, if their confession is sufficiently psychological or strikes a sufficiently heartfelt and authentic note of sincerity. Oh, we are sincere. I do not deny it. I don't know anybody nowadays who is not sincere. Didi Lovell is the most sincere person I know: every time she crawls in bed with somebody else, she does so with the utmost sincerity. We are the most sincere Laodiceans who ever got flushed down the sinkhole of history."[13]

Sincerity is not the same as integrity, although the two have much in common, particularly insofar as they present images of wholeness. With integrity, one disciplines his baser instincts so that they can conform to his higher purposes. Integrity always takes the high road and is much more likely to inspire others than to seduce them. With sincerity, the direction is just the reverse; one alters what one sees to agree with what one feels. Hence, it is easy for a vicious sincerity to be formed in which higher values are sacrificed for lower pleasures. Sincerity, therefore, must be

[13] Walker Percy, *The Moviegoer* (New York: Popular Library, 1961), pp. 204–5.

aligned with wisdom and truth in order to be safeguarded against collapsing into a vice.

Voltaire's most celebrated work, *Candide,* is about an utterly candid and sincere youth whose naiveté amounts to a form of comical infantilism. Small wonder Rousseau held so strong a hatred for France's most trenchant satirist. *Candide* can also be viewed as a biting satire against Rousseau's philosophy, in which feelings alone can provide a reliable guide for authentic living.

True sincerity—wholeness, simplicity, and genuineness of character—is a most beautiful virtue. But sincerity itself is not the path to sincerity. That path is one of wisdom and truth, and the inspiration to embark on that path comes from reverence and humility. The virtue that is most easy to feign may also be the most difficult to obtain.

TEMPERANCE

A T BIRTH, in 1917, his recorded name was John Wilson. As a writer, he was known to the world as Anthony Burgess. "Anthony" was the name he took at confirmation; "Burgess" was his mother's maiden name. He came into the world to lower-middle-class parents in Manchester, England.

Tragedy struck early in his life. Both his mother and his only sibling were victims of the Spanish influenza epidemic. His father, on furlough from the military, came home one day in 1919 to make the harrowing discovery that his wife and daughter were dead. As Burgess writes in the first volume of his confessions: "I apparently was chuckling in my cot while my mother and sister lay dead on a bed in the same room."[1]

The deprivation of a mother left its mark on him. "I never had a mother", he laments. "I was not encouraged to express tenderness. I was reared emotionally cold. . . . I regret the emotional coldness that was established then and which, apart from other faults, has marred my work."[2]

The fact that he was a Catholic growing up in a Protestant environment, and was more Irish than English, gave him a sense of displacement that remained with him for the rest of his life. Although he regarded himself in his adult

[1] Anthony Burgess, *Little Wilson and Big God* (London: Heinemann, 1987), p. 18.
[2] Ibid., pp. 86–88.

years as a "renegade Catholic", he never lost his esteem for Catholicism and always maintained that the Church represented the true faith. It was Catholicism that provided Burgess the perspective he needed in order to write about the human predicament in cosmic terms. "For Catholicism is, in a paradox, a bigger thing than the faith. It is a kind of nationality one is stuck with for ever. Or, rather, a supranationality that makes one despise small patriotisms."[3] Catholic theology, particularly that of Augustine, consistently informed his view of the world and man's nature. He could find no intellectual substitute for the Church: "I know of no other organisation that can both explain evil and, theoretically at least, brandish arms against it."[4]

He received his B.A. with honors, in English language and literature, in 1940 from the University of Manchester. He had taken his final examinations in a glass-roofed gymnasium on a day when Nazi bombers, on a daring daylight raid, had inflicted significant damage on Manchester.

Two years later, he married. Misfortune, however, was not far off. In 1944, while in London, his wife was assaulted by four vagrant men. Their intent was robbery. Having taken her purse, they tried to remove her wedding ring. As she screamed, they struck her, repeatedly. Pregnant at the time, Llewela lost the child. In addition, her injuries were severe enough to prevent her from having any more children. Burgess's best-known work, *A Clockwork Orange,* is based on this frightful incident. At the same time, the work raises a basic philosophical question concerning good and evil, freedom and control. Is it better, the book asks, for man to be free even though he will inevitably choose evil, or to be

[3] Ibid., p. 148.
[4] Ibid., p. 149.

controlled, as by behavioral scientists, and rendered incapable of choosing evil? Burgess's own preference is solidly with the former. No original sin, no evil. No evil, no moral choice. No moral choice, and human freedom becomes meaningless and man becomes a machine. Burgess sides with Augustine and original sin against the fourth-century heretic Pelagius, who asserted that man is perfectible through his own efforts. Burgess himself refers to *A Clockwork Orange* as "a sermon on the power of choice".[5]

The pivotal point in Burgess's life came in 1959 while he was teaching in Borneo in his capacity as an education officer for the British Colonial Service. After lecturing on the Boston Tea Party, he suddenly collapsed on the lecture-room floor. There was prompt action. He was taken to a local hospital, where a fellow graduate of Manchester University examined him. He was then flown back to England, to London's National Neurological Hospital, so that spinal taps could be taken. The spinal taps tentatively confirmed what the doctor in Borneo had suspected: an inoperable cerebral tumor. The doctors gave Burgess one year to live.

Burgess regarded his prognosis with a sense of relief. He had never been given a year to live before. He now had a whole year ahead of himself. "I wasn't going to be run over by a truck or drowned in the sea. I wasn't going to be knifed in Soho, and I was going to live for a year."[6] How would he spend that terminal year? His dominating concern was his wife, for he did not want to leave his prospective widow penniless. Although he had done little writing up to that point, and his life with the Colonial Service had

[5] "Anthony Burgess", *Contemporary Literary Criticism,* ed. D. G. Marowski (Detroit: Gage Researchers, 1986), vol. 40, p. 117.

[6] Rosemary Hartill, ed., *Writers Revealed* (New York: Peter Bedrick Books, 1989), pp. 17–18.

been shamelessly intemperate, he decided to use his final year to become a professional writer and provide income for Llewela.

The prospect of imminent death, as Samuel Johnson once said, "wonderfully concentrates the mind". Between November 1959 and the same month in the following year, he wrote five novels. Five "sterling" novels, as one critic has called them.[7] Unseduced by prospective death or the temptation to dissipation, he tempered himself and, sitting at his typewriter, transmuted black typeface into gold. It was a miraculous year, and when it ended, the "tumor" was gone and the talent triumphant. That year, as Burgess later reported, was probably the happiest of his life. He adopted a discipline that personified one of Aquinas's definitions of temperance, "serenity of the spirit" (*quies animi*). This discipline, in his words, "meant the production of two thousand words of fair copy everyday, weekends included".[8] It was a productive discipline that allowed him to consolidate his talents and energies as he had never done before.

Burgess never lost that discipline. When he died in 1993, he had published more than fifty books. But his range is even more impressive, including essays, literary criticism, books for children, motion-picture scripts, drama, short stories, translations, poetry, and a sizeable amount of serious musical compositions. A critic once made the following assessment of Burgess's productivity: "Anthony Burgess may be the most consummate professional writer now alive. His knowledge of literary, linguistic and musical arcana rivals that of any Oxford don; he writes with a

---

[7] Paul Boytinck, *Anthony Burgess, An Annotated Bibliography and Reference Guide* (New York: Garland Publishing, 1985), p. vii.

[8] Anthony Burgess, *You've Had Your Time* (London: Heinemann, 1990), pp. 4–5.

lyrical verve; and he seems willing to turn his hand to anything whatever."[9] Burgess's own summation of his life's work, which we find at the close of this two-part autobiography, is more temperate: "I have done my best, and no one can do more. I may yet have my time."[10]

Commentary

Temperance is the virtue that allows man to maintain his balance when the force of his bodily appetites threatens to violate the order of reason. These appetites, because they are associated with the desire for self-preservation, are deeply rooted in human nature and, consequently, can be very dangerous. The desire for self-preservation manifests itself on two levels: on the individual level in relation to food and drink; on the level of the species in relation to sex. The vice associated with the former is called "gluttony", while that associated with the latter is called "lust". Both gluttony and lust have a potentially destructive effect with respect to the integrity of the human personality.

Temperance should not be viewed merely as a form of moderation. Nor should it be reduced to the category of quantity. A person does not attain the virtue of temperance simply by avoiding excessive amounts of pleasurable gratifications. Temperance is not incompatible with exuberance and zestfulness. It is by no means a negative virtue (in fact, there are no negative virtues). Rather, it is the positive ordering of bodily appetites for the good of the whole person and others to whom he is related.

[9] Michael Dirda, "Anthony Burgess", *Contemporary Literary Criticism,* ed. D. G. Marowski (Detroit: Gale, 1986), 40: 119.
[10] Burgess, *You've Had Your Time,* p. 391.

The temperate person understands that obedience to reason is a greater good than the gratification of a single appetite. As Cicero has pointed out, "No man can be brave who thinks pain is the greatest evil; nor temperate, who considers pleasure the highest good."[11] Temperance, then, is a form of corporal piety based on the axiom that the order of the whole is superior to the isolation of the part.

Benjamin Franklin reflects an appreciation for the positive ordering of one's life that temperance permits when he writes: "Temperance puts wood on the fire, meal in the barrel, flour in the tub, money in the purse, credit in the country, contentment in the house, clothes on the children, vigor in the body, intelligence in the brain, and spirit in the whole constitution." Temperance, therefore, is more a luxury than a deprivation, since it allows a person to enjoy so many things at the same time. It is more like a carefully integrated symphony than a bagpipe solo.

A Japanese proverb outlines, in three steps, the potentially destructive effect alcohol can have on an intemperate person:

> First the man—takes the drink,
> Next the drink—takes the drink,
> Then the drink—takes the man.

A retired baseball player, a member of the Hall of Fame, reached the point where he thought his drinking might have gotten a bit out of hand. He confesses that he would start his days with brandy, Kahlua, and cream, and then consume up to four bottles of wine in an afternoon. Before personal appearances he would "warm up", to borrow a baseball metaphor, with three or four vodkas before he went to the cocktail party where he would have three or

[11] Cicero *De Officiis* I.2.

four more drinks.[12] He decided to quit drinking, not because he suddenly saw merit in temperance, but because he feared that he would be remembered only as a drunk. Needless to say, sobriety founded on the fear of soiling one's reputation is no more virtuous than the miser's abstemiousness on the grounds that a drinking habit would be incompatible with his greed.

Temperance is not a sign of boredom. It is not the mark of a dull personality. What it indicates is a preference for discipline over dissolution, maintenance over mayhem, balance over banality. To borrow from baseball lore once again, the temperate person is the "complete player", a Willie Mays at the height of his career. The intemperate person is a "designated hitter" who has been in a prolonged "batting slump".

The temperate person is simply more effective and productive than his intemperate counterpart. He is more full of life, even if he is ignored by the media or does not quantify his libidinal exploits in a "shocking" and "sensational" autobiography. As a direct result of his temperance, he enjoys a serenity of spirit that is the envy of those who lack temperance.

Traditional moralists understood that temperance was so fundamental and far-ranging that they accorded it a rather high place in the lexicon of virtues. It was considered a cardinal virtue, from the Italian root *cardine,* meaning "hinge". The cardinal virtues were like hinges that allowed the door to open to many other virtues. Temperance is needed so that there can be chastity, continence, humility, meekness. Without temperance there is lust, incontinence, pride, and

---

[12] *Toronto Globe and Mail,* April 16, 1994, p. D4.

unbridled wrath. Among the four cardinal virtues, prudence looks to all reality; justice to one's fellowman; fortitude is self-possession in a sea of danger; temperance is self-possession during a storm of passion.

Temperance is a "selfless self-preservation".[13] It is radically different from a "selfish self-preservation" because it is not fixed upon itself or limited to itself ("Whoever fixes his eyes on himself gives no light").[14] Selfless self-preservation represents an inner ordering of one's appetites, but with a view to becoming, not a kind of olympic model of virtue, an object of admiration, but an integrated human being whose talents and abilities can be directed to the good of others. Selfless self-preservation affirms the self without excluding others. By concentrating exclusively on the isolated self, selfish self-preservation results in self-destruction. Modern psychologists as well as contemporary writers have been tireless in pointing out that self-centeredness is a common source of neurotic anxiety. "For anyone who tries to preserve his life will lose it."[15]

[13] Josef Pieper, *The Four Cardinal Virtues* (New York: Harcourt, Brace and World, 1965), pp. 147–52.

[14] Ibid., p. 148.

[15] Lk 17:33. For parallel texts see Mt 10:39; 16:25; Mk 8:35; Lk 9:24.

WISDOM

YAHWEH APPEARED to King Solomon in a dream and said to him, "Ask what you would like me to give you." Solomon did not make his request immediately. Instead, he spoke at some length, expressing to God his reflections as a young king faced with the formidable responsibility of ruling a multitude of people so large in number as to be beyond reckoning. Finally, he made his request: "Give your servant a heart to understand how to discern between good and evil, for who could govern this people of yours that is so great?"[1] Then Yahweh said, "Since you have asked for this and not asked for long life for yourself or riches or the lives of your enemies, but have asked for a discerning judgment for yourself, here and now I do what you ask. I give you a heart wise and shrewd as none before you has had and none will have after you."[2] He asked but one thing of Solomon, to show fidelity to the beliefs and traditions of Israel.

The things Solomon expressed to God make it clear that he was well disposed to receive the divine gift of wisdom. The manner in which he made his request proved he already possessed numerous virtues, ensuring that his newfound wisdom would not be given in vain. The young king began by showing *gratitude* and *piety* for God's kindness to

[1] 1 Kings 3:9.
[2] 1 Kings 3:10–14.

his beloved father, King David. In addressing "Yahweh my God", and referring to himself as a "servant", he expressed *reverence* and *humility*. When he told of his great concern to rule his people well, he demonstrated the virtues of *care* and *justice*. By asking only for an understanding heart with the confidence that God would give it to him, he displayed *modesty* and *faith*. He also manifested *loyalty* and *determination* by pledging to remain faithful to God and persevering as a good ruler. At the same time, by not requesting long life, wealth, and death for his enemies, he revealed that he was not driven by the vices of selfishness, greed, and revenge.

How unlike Solomon are Plato's poor cave dwellers. In his famous analogy of the cave, Plato draws the image of prisoners wasting their lives looking at shadows that appear on the wall of the cave. He has a certain sympathy for these unfortunate creatures but understands, given their deprivation of light (both intellectually and morally), their radical indisposition against being liberated. "And would they not", Plato asks, "kill anyone who tried to release them and take them up, if they could somehow lay hands on him and kill him?"[3]

Solomon recognized the value of wisdom because he was virtuous. And virtues constituted the fertile soil in which wisdom could take root. The light of God's wisdom, as it were, was already reflected in his conduct. For Plato's visually and morally deprived cave dwellers, on the other hand, wisdom was alien and untrustworthy. Therefore, they steeled themselves against it. They lacked the virtues that would have allowed them to be open and receptive to

---

[3] Plato *Republic* 7.516b–517b. Here Plato may be alluding to the death of Socrates (see *Apology* 38d–41a).

wisdom. They could not will their liberation because they were ignorant of their need for it.

The wisdom God granted Solomon has three fundamental characteristics: it is a gift of divine origin; it is a unifying principle for all virtues; and it is a personal and interior power, not something impersonal and exterior as it is found in law. The fact that Yahweh appeared to Solomon in a dream is significant, because before the prophetic period, dreams were one of God's main channels of communication with man.

One way in which Solomon expressed his wisdom was through literature. One thousand and five songs are attributed to him.[4] The "sweetest" of his songs, about twenty-five of them, are found in the Song of Songs. Their popularity at wedding festivities established them so firmly in Israelite life that they were eventually admitted to the rank of Sacred Scripture on the ground that the songs present an allegory of the covenant between Yahweh and his people. They also reinforce notions basic to Israel's faith: God's intention that a man should live before him as a complete personality, that man and woman should find fulfillment in their union with each other, and that married love should partake of the goodness of creation.

To Solomon are also ascribed the book of Proverbs, Ecclesiastes, and Psalms 72 and 127. Apart from these sections of the Hebrew Bible, the Wisdom of Solomon, the Psalms of Solomon, and the Odes of Solomon are also attributed to him.

But by far the most important way in which Solomon manifested his wisdom was through the administration of justice. The most famous illustration of his wisdom in this

[4] 1 Kings 4:32.

regard was his adroit handling of the two women who claimed the same baby. According to the story, Solomon proposed to settle the dispute by cutting the baby in two with a sword, giving half to one woman and half to the other. At this point the real mother of the child offered to surrender the baby, and Solomon, with psychological understanding of a mother's love, rendered his verdict in her favor. In response to demonstrations of wisdom of this sort, the community responded with glowing praise and admiration: "And all Israel heard of the judgment which the king had rendered; and they stood in awe of the king, because they perceived that the wisdom of God was in him, to render justice."[5]

Solomon became renowned for his wisdom. When the Queen of Sheba came to visit him from far-off Arabia, she tested his wisdom. When she concluded her series of tests, she not only affirmed the accuracy of the reports that had come to her of his wisdom but said to him, "Your wisdom and prosperity surpass the report which I heard." She regarded as exceedingly fortunate those who "heard your wisdom" and pronounced blessed the Lord who "made you king, that you may execute justice and righteousness".[6]

Commentary

Serious-minded thinkers were once called wise men. Pythagoras, recognizing that in the strict sense wisdom belongs to God alone, coined the word "philosophy" (love of wisdom). He preferred to be known as a "lover of wisdom" than as a

[5] 1 Kings 3:28.
[6] 1 Kings 10:6–9.

"wise man". His modesty itself was a sign of great wisdom, for it is presumptuous, given the weakness of human nature in the face of the highest truths, for a person to think that he could ever personify wisdom. Man, as a philosopher, is limited. Nonetheless, philosophy is wisdom insofar as it is accessible to human nature.

Wisdom as a gift of God is dependent on God's prerogative and man's receptivity. But even on a lower order, where it represents man's highest natural achievement, it still remains elusive and indefinable. The great Persian poet-astronomer Omar Khayyam found wisdom to be no more than an empty word:

> With them the seed of Wisdom did I sow,
> And with mine own hand wrought to make it grow;
> And this was all the Harvest that I reaped —
> "I came like Water, and like Wind I go."[7]

Another poet has described wisdom in equally elusive terms:

> Ask, who is wise? — You'll find the self-same man
> A sage in France, a madman in Japan;
> And here some head beneath a mitre swells,
> Which there had tingled to a cap and bells.[8]

Aquinas would have agreed with these two poets, but only partially. For the Angelic Doctor, wisdom is a vanity and is purely relative only when applied to the nothingness of man, but not when it refers to his glory. "The creature is a vanity", he writes, "in so far as it comes from nothingness,

---

[7] Omar Khayyam, "The Rubaiyat of Omar Khayyam (Excerpts)", trans. by Edward Fitzgerald in John Ciardi, ed., *How Does a Poem Mean?* (Boston: Houghton-Mifflin 1959), verse 7, p. 955.

[8] Thomas Moore, "The Sceptic".

but not in so far as it is an image of God."[9] Elsewhere he states, "The creature is darkness in so far as it comes out of nothing. But inasmuch as it has its origin from God, it participates in his image and this leads to likeness to him."[10] In yet another locus he maintains that "God cannot be the cause of a tendency to not-being. Rather the creature has this of itself, in so far as it has developed out of nothing."[11]

Rabbi Isaac, a third-century scholar, provides us with an important insight concerning the challenge one faces when looking for eternal values: "Significant experiences and genuine blessings—love, compassion, justice, brotherhood, peace— are not to be found in anything that can be measured from the eye."[12] According to an old Jewish proverb, a wise man hears one thing and understands two. It is the spiritual counterpart that offers the secret to wisdom, not the knowledge itself.

Wisdom is not knowledge as much as it is the ordering of knowledge. Or, as Aquinas states, "*Sapientia est ordinare* [It belongs to wisdom to order things]".[13] The story is told of a man who was asked to choose between knowledge and wisdom. If he chose knowledge he would know everything; if he chose wisdom he would know a few things well. The man chose knowledge, assuming that if he knew everything, he would also know what wise people

[9] Thomas Aquinas, *Questiones disputatae de caritate,* 1 ad 11.

[10] Thomas Aquinas, *Questiones disputatae de veritate,* 18, 2 ad 5.

[11] Thomas Aquinas, *Summa Theologiae* I, 104, 3 ad 1.

[12] Bernard Mandelbaum, *Choose Life* (New York: Random House, 1968), p. xiii.

[13] Thomas Aquinas, *Summa contra Gentiles* 1, 1. See also Aristotle, *Metaphysics* 1, 2 (982a18), trans. W. D. Ross: "For the wise man must not be ordered but must order."

know. Wisdom, however, eluded him, precisely because it is not any specific knowledge but its ordering to an ultimate good.

The modern world reveals its lack of wisdom by its exclusive preoccupation with the experiential, the factual, and the classifiable. As T. S. Eliot writes:

Where is the Life we have lost in the living?
Where is the wisdom we have lost in knowledge?
Where is the knowledge we have lost in information?
The cycles of Heaven in twenty centuries
Bring us farther from God and nearer to the Dust.[14]

We are surrounded by things: things to know, things to have, things to possess, things to get rid of. But there is no wisdom contained within things. According to an eighth-century Jewish parable, two neighboring merchants were engaged in conversation while business was at a standstill. "Look," one said, "there are no customers today. I sell vegetables; you sell linen. Let us exchange our merchandise." This they did, but it gained them nothing. Then one of the merchants had an inspiration. "This morning I studied a chapter in the Bible," he said, "and I know you studied a different one. You teach me your chapter and I will teach you mine . . . and we will then know *two* chapters each."[15]

To trade one thing for another on a material level does not add to one's treasure, whereas to trade stories on a spiritual level, is to gain something new without giving up what one formerly possessed. With spiritual economics, one cannot lose but only gain.

The grass may appear greener on the other side of the fence, or in the merchandise our neighbor is offering for

[14] T. S. Eliot, *The Complete Poems and Plays* 1909–1950 (New York: Harcourt, Brace and World, 1952), p. 96.
[15] Mandelbaum, p. xvi.

sale. Wisdom, however, requires a detachment from material things so that one can begin to appreciate the truth that operates on a higher plane.

Rabbi Hanina, a first-century teacher, compared wisdom to a deep well of cool, sweet water. People could not enjoy its refreshing nourishment until a wise man tied one small string to another, attached the concatenation to a pitcher, and then drew up the water for all to drink. In like manner, said the rabbi, did King Solomon use wisdom to tie one little story, parable, and metaphor to another until he clarified the meaning of wisdom.

EPILOGUE

IT WAS STATED in the Prologue that love was not included among the twenty-eight virtues presented in this book because love is the form of all virtues. This notion that love forms all virtues and therefore is not simply a virtue itself is sufficiently important to warrant reiteration and further elaboration.

Without love, what passes for virtue is not true virtue. It is "counterfeit" virtue, as Aquinas states.[1] One may consider the example of Horace's "courageous" miser. The Roman poet tells us that "he braves the sea, he crosses mountains, he goes through fire; in order to avoid poverty."[2] Likewise, Augustine writes: "The prudence of the miser, whereby he devises various roads to gain, is no true virtue; nor the miser's justice, whereby he scorns the property of another through fear of severe punishment; nor the miser's temperance, whereby he curbs his desire for expensive pleasures."[3]

Virtue that is not animated by love falls short of being true virtue. For this reason Aquinas states that "charity", the highest form of love, "is the mother and the root of all virtues inasmuch as it is the form of them all."[4] "Charity is

---

[1] Thomas Aquinas, *Summa Theologiae* II–II, 23, 7.

[2] Horace *Epist.* 1.1.45.

[3] Augustine, *Contra Julian,* 4.3.

[4] *Summa Theologiae,* I–II, 62, 4. "Sic enim carita est mater omnium virtutum et radix, inquantum est omnium virtutum forma."

compared to the foundation or root in so far as all other virtues draw their sustenance and nourishment therefrom."[5] It is that which "enfolds all virtuous activity".[6]

The examples from life and literature that illustrate this book's twenty-eight virtues were selected, by and large, because they are particularized expressions of love. The meaning of "the heart of virtue", in fact, is the love that is expressed in act or in deed. Therefore, the book is primarily concerned with true virtue rather than its mere semblance. It is concerned mainly with how love helps and fulfills man rather than how effective a technique might be in producing questionable results. Members of a crime syndicate might be bound to each other in loyalty but not necessarily to each other's good as human beings.

The apostle Paul rightly states that, "If I give away all I have and if I deliver my body to be burned, but have not love, I gain nothing."[7] In reading more of his familiar panegyric on love, we find that it embodies at least fifteen of our aforementioned virtues: "Love is patient [patience] and kind [care]; love is not jealous [generosity] or boastful [modesty]; it is not arrogant [graciousness] or rude [courtesy]. Love does not insist on its own way [humility]; it is not irritable [temperance] or resentful [piety]; it does not rejoice at wrong [compassion], but rejoices in the right [justice]. Love bears all things [courage], believes all things [faith], hopes all things [hope], endures all things [meekness]."[8]

The virtues that allow love to express itself as act orchestrate the fullness of the human personality. The integration of love and virtue provides a far more promising and

[5] Ibid., 23, 8 ad 2.
[6] Thomas Aquinas, Disputations, *De Virtutibus Cardinalibus,* 2.
[7] 1 Cor 13:3.
[8] 1 Cor 13:4–8.

exciting model for human beings than does the computer, the conditioned reflex, or the creature of political correctness. It is not an old model as much as it is an eternal one. But most importantly, it encourages people to dare to become the extraordinary beings created in the image of God that is their destiny.